FROM CAPTIVE TO CAPTOR

Breaking Free from Fear and Anxiety

KATIE RICHARDS

WESTBOW
PRESS®
A DIVISION OF THOMAS NELSON
& ZONDERVAN

WestBow Press books may be ordered through booksellers or by contacting:

WestBow Press
A Division of Thomas Nelson & Zondervan
1663 Liberty Drive
Bloomington, IN 47403
www.westbowpress.com
844-714-3454

ISBN: 978-1-6642-3043-9 (sc)
ISBN: 978-1-6642-3044-6 (hc)
ISBN: 978-1-6642-3042-2 (e)

Library of Congress Control Number: 2021907219

Print information available on the last page.

WestBow Press rev. date: 04/16/2021

CONTENTS

This book is dedicated first to the Lord, for His faithfulness in the hard times and the freedom He bought for us at Calvary.

I also dedicate it to my sweet husband, who pushed me to chase my dreams and share my testimony and who always helps me strive to be my best and points me back to Christ.

Lastly, I want to dedicate this book to all those who walked with me through the trying seasons of life and prayed for me. I would not be here without you. Thank you.

INTRODUCTION

Picture yourself standing in a train station where it is all at once crowded, loud, busy, and overwhelming. Although many surround you, you cannot help but feel covered in loneliness. The train stops, and you realize it looks familiar. You have taken it before, and although you dread the destination, you still get on because it is the only way you know to go. You take your same seat next to the same people. One's name is Fear; another is Worry. Across the aisle from you is Doubt and Doubt's friend Defeat. You lift your head to see who is in front of you, and once again, Anxiety is dressed in the brightest, most deafening attire. Depression sits next to him, sulking in the shadows. You turn and look out the window, knowing this trip leads into a darkening spiral that seems to never end. You know your fellow passengers will ask you the same questions:

"How can you go on living like this?"

"Who do you think you are?"

And the all-encompassing question, "What if …?"

Fear asks you, "What if you die from this? What if you will never be free of this?" He turns to Worry, who asks, "What if you cannot afford your bills when you get off? I have heard you aren't quite making enough these days. Not to mention—what if you never lose the baby weight? Surely you are worried if your husband will still find you attractive."

Doubt walks over and adds in his input: "Yeah, what if God never answers your prayer for healing, and what if God does not even hear your prayers? Surely if He heard your prayers, you would be off this ride. What if He does not even love you?"

You take a deep breath, anticipating Anxiety's and Depression's questions.

Anxiety asks, "What if you always take this trip? What if you never get off this ride? What if you never achieve anything in life?"

And Depression adds, "What if life is not worth the hassle? What if you never find hope for joy again? What if ... what if ... what if ...?"

This ride seems to take a lifetime, and you feel your reserves emptying. Exhaustion, weakness, loneliness, isolation, hopelessness, darkness—you feel as though there is no end in sight, yet the end is all you hope for.

The train stops and, relieved, you scurry off, hoping to be delivered from the heavy presence of Fear, Worry, Doubt, Anxiety, and Depression. As you look up to see where you are going, you realize you are in the same place from which you just left—busy, crowded, loud ... lonely. The train leaves, and you walk around. You see a path ahead but are not quite sure where it leads. Behind you, the next train arrives, which will take the same route to the same destination.

Do you get on again because it is what you know, or do you take the new path that is unknown but could lead to freedom?

I have been on that seemingly never-ending ride of fear, worry, anxiety, doubt, and depression. A ride that, though I hated the destination, I seemed to continuously get back on. No matter what I did, it felt like the train would arrive and I'd find myself seated again, being bombarded with the dreaded what-ifs.

It was not until I realized the root of my fears, worries, and doubts that I was able to find freedom from them. I realized the root of everything I struggled with stemmed from those two words: "What if?"

Even in your current place of hopelessness, anxiety, and constant worry, I want you to know that freedom is available to you. If you are a Christian who has walked with the Lord, and you have walked through a season of doubt and fear, there is hope. If you are not saved and have lived your whole life fighting with darkness, hope and salvation are available to you.

I have seen a pattern of our society accepting these things as a way of life—as a new normal. All too often, I see Christians, who profess to know the God of freedom, wallowing in the bondage of anxiety and fear and accepting them as a life sentence. Coming from a psychology background, I understand the science of the mind— the causes, effects, processes, and even diagnoses of some of the things we have grown comfortable living in. But I also understand the God I serve.

This is not a self-help book or a counseling technique to help you live with fear, anxiety, and depression by numbing its symptoms. Rather, it is a testimony of my freedom from anxiety and depression. A testimony of what is available to you so that you will not believe any longer the lie that you will always have to live this way. It is a testament of God's faithfulness and truth found in His Word and the revelations He gave me to be free in my mind.

I believe wholeheartedly in the study of God's creation of the mind. My undergraduate studies were in psychology and my master's studies were in counseling. I also wholeheartedly believe in the counseling process as a tool for God to bring about healing and wholeness to the broken. I don't intend to discount psychology and counseling, but I did achieve freedom without any medicine or counseling service by using the principles in this book—principles derived only from the Word of God.

Scripture says, "And you will know the truth, and the truth will set you free" (John 8:32 NLT). Jesus told them, "I am the Way, the Truth, the Life; no one can come to the Father except through Me" (John 14:6 NLT). And in John 1:1, we are told, "In the beginning [before all time] was the Word (Christ), and the Word was with God, and the Word was God Himself" (AMP).

All these scriptures show that truth is Christ and the Word

of God, and truth brings freedom. This book discusses the truth of God that brings freedom from anxiety and fear, demolishes strongholds built in our minds, and teaches us the way to truly have the mind of Christ.

PART 1

Foundations of Fear

CHAPTER 1
What Do We Fear?

One of the first ways to walk in freedom from fear is to understand exactly what you fear. When I first experienced anxiety, I felt confused because I could not quite pinpoint what was causing me to feel anxious. I just constantly felt afraid without having any specific reason for it. Have you ever felt that way? Have you ever woken up from a full night's sleep feeling anxious and not knowing why? I remember, during my battle with fear and anxiety, waking up with instant dread. My mind immediately would ask, *How do I already feel this way when I haven't even had my first thought of the day?*

One thing that God showed me was the foundations of why I felt anxious. You see, becoming fearful and anxious is not an overnight process; it is a lengthy process of developing fearful thinking patterns and accepting anxious thoughts without filtering them or aligning them with the Word of God.

You may wonder why you still battle fear and anxiety, even though you study the Word and go to church. I asked myself the same questions. I never battled anxiety as hard as when I felt closest to God. It didn't make sense, but that's just it—sometimes it won't. It wasn't that I wasn't saved or didn't love God, but I had a mind that I did not make obedient to Christ. I said the right things with my mouth but did not truly believe them and adhere to them in my mind.

My father and mother today are not the same people who raised me. I am thankful that God gave me parents who raised me to know of God, but because of their brokenness, I had a broken view of God. They both came from unstable homes that taught anxiousness, fear, and some misconstrued beliefs about the goodness of God. Thank God that both of my parents did so much better for us, but scars often transfer to our children if we do not heal ourselves. We see this in society through cycles of poverty, abuse, and addiction. God has now delivered and healed my parents completely, and I am honored to serve alongside them in ministry to heal the broken and to spread freedom to the nations. I only share the past because it is our past that shapes us and often shapes our ways of thinking. My past shows how I became broken, but it also glorifies God in His redemption and faithfulness.

My father was in the military, and those military attitudes and principles he applied to us would sometimes lead me to not feel good about my identity. I remember one time in particular when I took it upon myself to organize and clean out the kitchen cabinets. It took me about two hours, but I managed to organize all the spices, flours, and sugars, and I felt quite proud of myself when I was finished. When my father walked through the door after work, I was so excited to show him what I'd done.

"Look, Dad, I organized the cabinet!" I beamed as he came to look and waited for his affirmation of what a good job I did.

"It looks good," he said, "but you should have swept out the bottom first. It would have been better."

He did not intentionally mean to hurt me, but that moment left a note on my heart that said, "Not good enough." He didn't purposefully want to send that message, but when we filter all our words and interactions through brokenness, it can impact those around us. Because he wasn't healed from perfectionism, it passed down to me.

It sounds like a simple story, but this one particularly marked me. No matter what I did, I would not be good enough. If I made an A-, I'd ask, *Why didn't I make an A+?* If I scored a homerun, I'd ask, *Why didn't I score two?* For some, this mindset looks like not ever trying at anything because why try when you know you won't be good enough? For others, like me, this mindset appears in my attempts at perfectionism and often an overly competitive attitude.

I began to develop an understanding of God's character as well. He was a Father whom I could not please, and I needed His love and approval, earned through always doing everything right.

If we went back in time and you asked me if I believed that I could not please God and that He did not love me, I would have boldly proclaimed the opposite. Often, our mindsets and beliefs about God are at work at an unseen level, shaping our behaviors and thought lives in a way that sometimes goes unnoticed on the outside. But when these broken thought patterns are the root systems of our thought lives, they lead to fear, anxiety, and depression.

My mother was very anxious and cautious, often making decisions out of fear. If we children messed up, we were taught that God's wrath and punishment were not far away. The God about whom my mother taught us was a God whose hammer was ready to swing at the drop of a hat. She was not malicious or purposeful in teaching these lessons, but she taught us only what she herself believed about the Father. Her fear of raising her kids correctly for the Lord sometimes translated into being too strict and too cautious.

I was "saved" many times as a teenager due to believing His salvation was so easily removed by my mistakes. Although I spoke of His love and goodness, beneath the surface, I believed that God was a God of anger and wrath, and any step out of line would remove His love from me and lead to punishment. This was another root that allowed fear and anxiety to enter my mind.

I got officially saved the summer after my senior year of high school, prior to entering my first year of college. I'd been taught about God my whole life by my parents; I had been baptized and often preached God to everyone who had questions about Him in high school, but my life had not been surrendered to Him fully yet. Although I believe God's hand was on my life at an early age, I always say that I was saved in July 2012 because that is when I understood my personal need for salvation and the love of God in my life.

I was particularly broken at the time of my salvation. A young-love experience led me to forfeit my purity in a way that left me broken, thrown away, and worthless, in my mind. I grieved so deeply one night—grieved for the loss of a boy who did not love me, the loss of my virginity, the loss of my childhood, and the loss of everything I felt I knew. I could not remember the last time that I had eaten, laughed, or breathed without grief being present.

That night, I lay in my bed in a pit of despair. Although I could not find the words to pray, I believe my spirit prayed for me. Romans 8:26 (AMP) says,

> In the same way the Spirit [comes to us and] helps us in our weakness. We do not know what prayer to offer or how to offer it as we should, but the Spirit Himself [knows our need and at the right time] intercedes on our behalf with sighs and groanings too deep for words.

This was a moment when the Lord took over for me so that I could take my first step toward healing. When you don't know what to do, you can trust the Lord to lead you through your darkest moments.

Amid the broken spirit and turmoil of my soul, I didn't know how much more I could handle of the heaviness I was carrying. In that moment, the Lord did something for me that changed my life forever. He sent me the spirit of joy in my room, and I began to laugh and feel my soul lift a little. Although it did not last too long, it was enough light in my darkness to get me through another night. Realizing what had happened, I knelt in my bedroom and surrendered to God, and in that moment, I realized that even though

I had not "cleaned up" myself yet from the mess I had made, God still wanted me.

Up to that point, I believed that I needed to make myself good enough for Him before He would want me, but there He was, holding a hand out in the middle of my mess. I took His hand and never looked back, and I began to realize that He loved me and wanted me for *me*, and not for what I could do for Him. That is when I sold out to Him. From then on, I would live for Him, and my journey with Him truly began that night.

Psalm 40:2 (AMP) says, "He brought me up out of a horrible pit [of tumult and of destruction], out of the miry clay, and He set my feet upon a rock, steadying my footsteps and establishing my path." If you feel like you are stuck in your own place of destruction and miry clay, He will always be there to lift you up when you turn toward Him.

In that moment, I realized a truth about God's character: He loved me unconditionally and wanted me as I was. But that thought had to combat the many years of lies I had believed about Him—lies that told me I would never be good enough, that I had to earn His love, and that He was a Father who punished rather than gave good gifts. But that small touch of unconditional love that He showed me that night pushed me toward Him, and I began my journey, looking forward to my future rather than dreading it.

My freshman year of college was a blast. I developed new friends, experienced new adventures, and began to grow in God and as a person. When I was getting ready to go home that first summer, however, I just felt like something bad was going to happen. I don't know why I felt that way, but I wasn't looking forward to not having college, which kept me from the memories of home. Home reminded me of the hard summer I had gone through, full of depression and difficult memories.

When people speak of first heartbreaks, they never mention the time it takes sometimes to heal. College was a great distraction from things I did not want to deal with yet. I truly believed I was no longer attached to my first love, but that proved untrue when all distractions were pushed aside.

One night at my best friend's home, we watched a video, and I heard a familiar voice, one I had not heard for quite some time. My heart panged and broke a little, and I realized that a remnant of what I had hoped was gone was still in my heart. I had learned about spiritual bonds and soul ties in church, and I realized that although I felt that I had moved on, I had a spiritual tie to my first love that still remained from losing my purity before marriage. This is one reason the Lord purposes sex for the covenant of marriage—because it is never meant to be broken, and when it is, it takes time to heal. When we step outside of His plans, we create ties with people that we were never meant to make, and we can carry those ties with us into our next relationships, into our marriages, whether we know it or not.

It is so important that you seek freedom from soul ties to any past relationships so that you can move forward, baggage-free, into the relationship that God has planned for you. If you have made that mistake and given yourself to someone who did not hold you sacred and cherished, God can heal your wounds and place you back on the path He has for you. He has a great track record of making broken things quite beautiful in time.

I went home that night, sat in my bed, and prayed aloud: "God, please remove all soul ties and emotional bonds that I have. Please let me be free and move forward in the plans that You have for me." I felt really good and holy about the prayer, but I had no idea that a hard test would be waiting for me in the morning. I woke up to a text message from the one I never thought I would speak to again. The text was two or three paragraphs and spoke about a dream he'd had of me marrying another man. In the dream, he was standing at the back of a huge chapel, watching the wedding and crying because he knew he had messed up.

My heart leaped for joy at the words, and hope flooded my soul. A smile beamed on my lips, and tears welled in my eyes. Maybe God was changing his heart; maybe God had a plan and purpose. Rather than take a step back and let the Holy Spirit speak in that moment, I allowed my flesh speak to me. I texted back, and the test began. We met up a few times and talked about old times, reigniting a flame that was never meant to burn. Everything was looking great—and then my mother spoke to me.

I had come home from his graduation and walked into the kitchen, smiling. My mother came in behind me and simply said, "Really? Are you serious?"

My heart sank, my rose-colored glasses shattered, and my ear inclined to the Spirit for the first time in the situation. Dread filled my soul because I knew what needed to be done. I knew what God had planned for my life, and it didn't have the person included in it. Although he was not a bad person, and I believe truly cared for me at some level, not every relationship is meant to be forever. We were on different paths, and I needed to walk in the other direction.

If you feel that God is leading you out of something, it is OK to walk away. Trust the Lord and His purposes. I promise they are always better than our own plans.

I asked myself, "What in the world was I thinking? Why did I even entertain the idea of getting back together with him?" I cried in my bed that night, asking God what was wrong with me.

And He simply answered, "It isn't broken yet, but it can be."

In that moment, I knew that I needed to pray the will of the Father, but my flesh fought against me. My lips could barely utter what I wanted to say, and I knew that if I prayed, "Your will be done," that I would have to give up what my flesh wanted. That night was the first night that I ever felt anxiety.

Fear flooded my soul—fear of the future, fear of my heart breaking again, fear of what God would do if I continued seeing him, just crippling fear. It kept me up that night, and I battled between flesh and spirit. Finally, I forced myself to pray, "Your will be done," and got ready to end things. Anxiety stayed with me until I cut things off and then settled, once it was done. That was when the first root of fear set itself up in my mind.

This was the lie that I believed: that God gave me anxiety because I was out of His will, and He would not take it away until I was obedient. This caused me to build in my mind a stronghold of beliefs that led me to irrationally fear disobeying God. I did not want to feel that anxiety again, so I was stringent on not disobeying Him in any way, especially in my relationships. None of this was reality, but it was what I allowed my mind to believe about God. I carried it with me from that moment forward.

What really happened was that my spirit knew that what I was doing was not good for me, and the fear that I would be heartbroken again if I continued made me anxious. Instead of labeling the anxiety as knowing I walked down a dangerous path, I labeled it as something God had given me to tell me what to do. If I had been strong in the Word, I would have known that God does not give fear, and I would have been able to demolish that thought right away.

> For God did not give us a spirit of timidity or cowardice or fear, but [He has given us a spirit] of powder and of love and of sound judgment and personal discipline [abilities that result in a calm, well-balanced mind and self-control]. (2 Timothy 1:7 AMP)

Had I done what the Word says and renewed my mind and taken captive every thought that came against the knowledge of Christ (the Word), then I could have told that lie that it wasn't true and wasn't welcome; that God did not give me fear but gave me power, love, and self-discipline. However, I permitted that thought to remain in my mind and allowed the enemy territory. That was when the stronghold of anxiety was built, and upon that lie, another formed, as I continuously played the experience over and over in my mind.

The second lie was that because I had sinned and was disobedient in my relationship, God had taken away a person I loved. Thus, if I was disobedient to God in my relationships, He would take people I loved out of my life. Rather than fight against this lie with the Word, I allowed it to remain, and the stronghold grew stronger, and anxiety grew another root in my soul.

I craved being married to a godly man so that I could start my ministry, family, and life, yet at the same time, I feared stepping into another relationship. What if I chose wrong? What if I had anxiety again? What if I got hurt? What if ... what if ... what if ...?

This was how the root of my anxiety began. From believing God was a punisher, unpleasable, and unreachable to believing He gave fear and anxiety and wanted to take good things from me, my life experiences shaped and molded strongholds and root systems of fear in my life and mind. Had I known the Word and allowed the Word to renew my mind, I could have missed the battle with anxiety that was looming on the horizon. But when we allow lies to take hold and do not fight against them, we allow the enemy to take up territory in our lives.

Anxiety and fear built roots in my life through my childhood and relationships. If you are dealing with anxiety and fear, take a moment to think about some experiences that might have led to you believe some lies, which could have led to a stronghold of fear. What are lies you believe about God, yourself, and others? What are lies you have not taken captive, that the enemy uses against you to bombard you with fear and anxiety?

The first step to combating fear in your life is allowing God to reveal to you what you fear. As we go forward in this journey, you will see how those roots grew fruit in my life. As I continued in my relationship with God, He continued to prune away at those roots, which brought fear and anxiety to the surface and ultimately led to me having to face those lies. It was time that I let God weed my mind and remove rotten fruits that were unhealthy and damaging to me.

CHAPTER 2
The Fruit of the Roots

Roots produce fruit. If you've ever pulled weeds from a garden for what feels like 1,500 times in one season, then you understand this reality. The thing is, weeds will continue to grow amid beautiful flowers if they have roots and seeds. That is what roots of fear, anxiety, depression, and other things are like. Even though they may be growing amid good fruits of the spirits, like joy, peace, and self-discipline, if they are continuously allowed to grow, they will flourish. In gardens where weeds are allowed to flourish, they eventually smother the other blooms, leaving you with a dead, weedy garden.

We can chase after beautiful fruits in our lives all day long, but as long as we continue to allow certain roots to grow and stay in our minds, those fruits will become smothered by weeds. Luke 8:14 says, "The seed which fell among the thorns, these are the ones who have heard, but as they go on their way are suffocated with the anxieties and riches and pleasures of this life, and they bring no fruit to maturity" (AMP).

I had continued to grow deeper in my relationship with God and experienced His presence in my life in such a beautiful way, but any time I ventured toward thinking about having a romantic relationship, anxiety chased me away. I would go on a date and leave feeling so anxious that I also felt physically ill. I would say to myself,

"If I feel anxiety, it must be because that person is not from God," and then I would flee. Even if the person was a godly guy, I would run the instant anxiety hinted in my heart. For about four straight years, I remained single, even though my heart craved the one the Lord had purposed for me. I just could not break free from fear.

Many canceled dates and relationships later, I developed a close friendship with a very nice guy. We grew even closer after he moved back home, a good distance away, and I found I really cared for him. I was just beginning my senior year of college when we decided to try to take things to the next level. I was excited because he was godly and funny, and we had many things in common. We "dated" for about a month or two—it was long distance, and we only went on one real date.

One day in particular, when I was driving home from school, I felt so full of joy. Finally, things were going right in my life. School was great, my family was great, and my relationship was headed for good things. That night, I sat down and watched a faith-based documentary about a man in Japan who had a ministry that helped abandoned babies. It moved me so greatly, and I thought, *Wow, what I wouldn't do to surrender like that to God and serve Him in whatever He asked me to do!*

Infused with a sense of passion and excitement for God's plans in my life, I decided to pray a bold prayer when I lay down for bed that night. "God," I said, "I will do whatever you ask me to do." My motives for that prayer were positioned toward ministry, so I wasn't prepared for the immediate answer I received from the Father. "Give him up." Did I hear that right? Did God just ask me to give up my boyfriend? Are you kidding me?

Immediately, the familiar feeling gripped my heart again. There it was, suffocating me. I knew it would be back. What if I had misheard? What if that was just fear telling me to run again? What if I ruined what God had planned because of anxiety? What if I never got married because I always had anxiety? What if … what if … what if …? I lay in my dark room and began to weep. Not again. Years of battling anxiety every time I tried to date had led me to exhaustion. I finally had begun to hope again when I was dealt this hard blow.

I took a day to make sure that I had heard God, and after much prayer and seeking godly wisdom and counsel, I decided to do as God asked and give up the relationship. Luckily, he understood and even said that he had felt like he should have set things on hold for some time to focus on God. Breathing a sigh of relief, I immediately felt better and believed once again the lie that anxiety was the tool God used in my life to guide me to right relationships.

The next day, I went to lunch with my best friend (she'd been my best friend for about nine years at that time, and she is still my best friend to this day; she is a direct blessing from God). We had been friends throughout high school and became roommates in college, and although we had been through some ups and downs, her relationship was important to my life. As I drove home from lunch, listening to a devotional CD, the pastor speaking on the CD made a single statement that began a domino effect of anxiety and fear. She said that to delay obedience to God was the same as disobedience to Him.

Disobedience. *Disobedience.* It rang in my ear like a chapel bell, and I ruminated on it over and over again. Dread and anxiety filled my soul, and I felt panic grip my heart. *Oh no, I waited a day to break up with my boyfriend. What if God thinks that was disobedience? What if God takes away my best friend because I was disobedient to Him by waiting to do what He asked me to do?*

You might be thinking that was an irrational thing to believe about God. But the fruits of the roots I had allowed to grow in my mind and had never dealt with finally broke through the ground. My beliefs—about God taking people I loved from my life if I was disobedient—came to the surface. My fear that God would give me anxiety to tell me when to break off relationships cluttered my mind.

I immediately felt nauseated. The war had begun. Now, I was at an impasse. I either had to end my friendship with Abby in order to alleviate the anxiety (said the lie), or I had to stay in this prison of panic and anxiety, fearing being disobedient to God. Up to this point, it had been easy to break off relationships when anxiety reared its ugly head—although I'd had some feelings for those people, they were very early relationships, which were easier to end.

But now, here was anxiety, trying to take my best friend away. My soul sister. The girl who had walked with me through so many trials and hard times; the girl whom God had given to me—I knew that in my soul—as a blessing and lifetime relationship. I was in a battle, finally coming face-to-face with the stronghold of lies that had been growing in my mind and the stronghold of truths I knew about God.

It was time to deal with the things I had allowed myself to believe about God. Time to be free of anxiety and fear. I wish I could tell you that it was an overnight process, and that I knew for a fact that God was not asking me to give up Abby, and that I immediately broke free of anxiety and walked in peace from that day forward. That was not the case. My freedom was a slow and steady process of allowing God to renew my mind.

I will share with you what I learned and how I became free.

When roots grow, they branch out and grow stronger. As they go deeper and deeper, they fortify the plant so that it cannot be easily plucked out or blown over. When we allow lies of the enemy about God, ourselves, and others to be rooted in our minds, it takes some time to remove them. Often, the task of weeding our gardens (minds) is so hard that we simply give up and allow them to overgrow the garden.

My friend, if you want to be free of anxiety and fear and all the other lies that have taken root in your mind and heart, it is time to do some work.

That day of awakening was painful. The process of becoming

free of anxiety was painful. It turned into a week of panic attacks that led me to the hospital, and that week turned into two years of numbing anxiety and darkness. As God exposed one lie, another came to the surface, and all at once, I found myself in the midst of a storm, surrounded by a hurricane of lies coming from every direction.

"You're disobeying God by staying friends with her. Remember? You have anxiety? That means run!"

"Your life will be run by anxiety forever. You want a husband? Too bad! Next time you try to date, anxiety will take him away too."

"You will never have a family because you're going to let anxiety steal everything from you."

"God doesn't love you, or He wouldn't let you go through this. What kind of good Father would allow His children to stay in this darkness?"

"You are never going to be free from fear. You might as well end it now."

"There is no hope for your future. There is only fear."

The enemy tried everything in his power to steal my joy, my hope, and even my life. I felt hopeless. He threw every lie that had any merit against my roots, and God allowed him to throw those lies because, at the same time, God was teaching me how to have a mind like Christ, how to take captive every thought, and how to renew my mind.

For some time, the fear of disobedience gripped my heart so heavily that I even feared going to the Word of God, in fear that I would read a scripture that might remind me of disobedience. I was working at a coffee shop during that time, but it had very few customers, so I did my course work and often read whatever books I had brought with me. My Bible sat on the counter next to me, often screaming at me that it held hope, while lies screamed that it held more anxiety and fear.

As I had done many years ago, I fought my flesh with the spirit and made myself read the Word, no matter how uncomfortable.

Although I had roots of fear, I also had roots of faith that believed the Word was truth, and with truth came freedom. I read every line of scripture, even with anxiety welling up inside me. I wish I could say that I felt better instantly, but I didn't. Instead, I grew steadfast in that time, learning that no matter what my flesh felt, my spirit would prevail in God and in faith.

One day, I was in my room, studying the Word, exhausted from my daily battle with anxiety and fear—just so exhausted. I was reading a version of the Word that dives deeper into the Greek and Hebrew meanings in the text to offer a better understanding of what scriptures. I was reading scripture on fear and anxiety, hoping for freedom again, when I came across 1 John 4:18. I had read this verse plenty of times before: "Perfect love casts out fear" (KJV). What a beautiful sentiment, but it didn't really help in my case.

Up to this point, I did not realize any of the roots that were showing in my life. What I've told you thus far came through the wisdom and understanding of God, but that was not present during my battle. Every day, I battled anxiety, even though I didn't understand where it came from; I was a victim of a battle in which I believed I had no fight.

When I read 1 John 4:18 with a deeper understanding of its meaning, God revealed—for the first time—a root.

> There is no fear in love [dread does not exist]. But perfect (complete, full-grown) love drives out fear, because fear involves [the expectation of divine] punishment, so the one who is afraid [of God's judgement] is not perfected in love [has not grown into a sufficient understanding of God's love]. (1 John 4:18 AMP)

When my eyes saw those words, I felt a root break in my soul. My mind danced in this new revelation of God. *Wait—God doesn't give me fear? Everything I have faced is because I don't understand His love?* Finally, I understood why I was battling anxiety; it was because I didn't know how God loved me yet! Hope soared through my soul. I beamed with praise for God because He allowed me to know this truth. Although fear and anxiety did not immediately leave me, that day was a turning point in my battle. A root had been exposed, which allowed the Gardener to know where to begin pruning and plucking. Although I still didn't have all the answers, I knew where to start. I needed to learn about God's love for me.

The fruit of the roots we allow to grow in our minds will appear at some point. What we allow to simmer under the surface will raise its ugly head. Whether it's anger, lust, fear, anxiety, or whatever you've been hanging on to and allowing to take root, it doesn't just go away because you don't think about it. Like a bullet left under the skin, it festers and irritates, revealing its scars and bruises over and over until it is finally uprooted.

The fruit of the roots that I had allowed to grow attempted to take away my godly relationships, my peace, and my joy. The enemy's plan was to cause me to run rather than fight for what I knew God had intended for my life. Where I had run before, now I fought for my best friend. Eventually, that fear left, regarding her, specifically; that battle had been won. But it wasn't over. Because God had something planned that He needed me to fight through, the final battle with fear and anxiety was on its way.

But God doesn't allow us to fight for no reason. He knows what's ahead and what He has waiting for us. Often, the battles of today are preparations for the next season that He is taking us into tomorrow. Had I not fought and instead surrendered to fear, I would not have developed the skills necessary to battle for my husband in the future. Had God just instantly delivered me when I first prayed, I would not have learned how to cast down every thought the enemy threw at me and renew my mind.

Sometimes, we want an easy way out, but just as a spoiled child who is always handed things never learns hard work, a Christian who never battles never learns how to walk in this life victoriously.

The fruits of the roots of your fear, anxiety, depression, and current struggles are signs that it is time to begin work in your garden. Don't run from the symptoms and medicate them. Don't numb them with busyness, relationships, or entertainment. Face them. When fruits start appearing, it isn't time to be afraid of the battle ahead but to trust that the Gardener is ready to begin making you beautiful.

What fruits do you see playing out in your life? What things do you believe are symptoms of roots you have allowed to grow for too long? Don't lose hope. For where there is brokenness, we can trust there is a Restorer who knows how to make things beautiful in their own time.

Isaiah 61:1–3 says,

> The Spirit of the Lord God is upon Me, Because the Lord has anointed Me to preach good tidings to the poor; He has sent Me to heal the brokenhearted, to proclaim liberty to the captives, and the opening of the prison to those who are bound; to proclaim the acceptable year of the Lord, and the day of vengeance of our God; to comfort all who mourn, to console those who mourn in Zion, *to give them beauty for ashes, the oil of joy for mourning, the garment of praise for the spirit of heaviness*; that they may be called trees of righteousness, the planting of the Lord, that He may be glorified. (NKJV, emphasis added)

We have a God who is the Master at making things new. He has perfected the art of restoring broken things, mending messes, and replanting souls. I love that this scripture calls the act of restoration "the planting of the Lord." Although the enemy likes to plant roots of darkness, like fear, anxiety, depression, and bitterness, we have a more powerful God, who can plant righteousness, joy, peace, love, and wholeness.

Do not lose hope, for the Gardener has come to make your

garden a place of peace and solace that will bear only the fruits of the Spirit that bring God glory. It is hard work to allow God to uproot things that are not of Him; it hurts, and you may feel like your foundations have been shaken. But trust the Lord; it is worth it.

~

CHAPTER 3
Broken for a Season

Right before fear took a major hold in my life, I thought everything was going pretty well. The summer before my senior year of college, I got to travel for the first time in my life. I boarded an airplane for an eleven-hour flight (what a great way to start) to Europe! What an adventure it was! Traveling was such a wonderful experience. I finally got to see the world and caught the travel bug; I knew that, one day, God would use this love for His purposes.

When I returned home, I went on vacation with my best friend to Florida and had the time of my life. It was such a fond trip with sweet memories, great friends, and much laughter. Later that summer, I also went on my first camping trip ever in the Great Smoky Mountains. Besides sleeping five feet away from a black bear (that's a story for another time), I had a great trip, enjoying the beautiful mountains and the friends God had blessed me with.

I felt that I was in a perfect time in my life. I had a great group of friends, and the pieces of my life's puzzle finally seemed to be coming together. I thought I only needed a boyfriend, and life would be great! Of course, it was after this summer that I got the boyfriend God asked me to surrender, which led me to the path of fear and anxiety. (Be careful what you wish for.)

It felt like, in a second, my life had gone from beautiful to broken. The thought, *Everything in my life is going well*, suddenly switched to, *Everything in my life is falling apart.* What had been on the back burner of my life all came forward. As I entered into a fight with fear and anxiety, it felt as though my family was falling apart as well. My siblings went through divorces and hard life struggles. My mother took to the only answer she knew—fear and anxiety—and my father numbly walked through it as he attempted to hold the family together.

As the only child who had it all together, I felt guilty if I needed to lean on my parents for any help, so, much of the time, I tried to battle all by myself. I didn't want to add any more to their plates. I didn't feel like I had anyone to turn to during that season because no one had gone through it before; it was very much a season of loneliness as well.

During that time, God was opening doors in my life for ministry purposes. I had been working with a nonprofit that worked with victims of child sex trafficking, and I volunteered often with that group because it was a heavy burden on my heart. As my graduation approached, they asked me to consider moving to Guatemala for a time to help run the program while the current leader went on maternity leave.

I went home that night and battled very hard. Part of me knew, without a doubt, that this was a God door; the other part of me believed the lie that I was too broken to serve anybody. I thought, *I can barely hold myself together. Why in the world would I try to hold someone else together?* But God works in very mysterious ways. If you have served Him for any time, you understand this notion.

I have learned to accept my own personality. I am a type-A, anal-retentive, super-organized, perfectionistic person—and that has often served me well in many arenas. More often, however, I have found myself praying for a different personality. "Lord, please let me be more laidback like so-and-so," or "Lord, please let me not care so much."

Parts of my personality have helped me through my toughest seasons. My stubbornness does not let me give up, no matter how bleak the circumstances may appear. Although I was afraid to make the commitment to go to Guatemala on my own in the midst of the strongest storm in my life, I also was too stubborn to let fear ruin what God was trying to do. I made a statement that got me through the entire event: "If I have to go in a straitjacket, I am going."

I boarded the plane two weeks after graduating college and flew to a third-world country for the first time in my life. Over the next three months, what I learned changed my path in life forever. One story sums up a major lesson that I still cling to today.

The girls in Guatemala lived in a government home that took in specifically trafficked or abused children, from infants to eighteen years of age. As is often the case, head lice was a known obstacle for those who lived there. Even if we rid the home of lice for a week, new incoming girls often brought them in. No one had warned me about lice—maybe they thought it was common knowledge—and this was my first time in that type of environment.

On one of the first times we visited the home, I prayed closely with more than ten girls, embracing them, crying with them, letting them rest their heads on my shoulders. It was a beautiful moment of intimacy with the Lord and watching His healing hand. The next week, however, I looked in the mirror and saw something strange in my bangs. Panicking, I called a volunteer, who checked and gave me the news: "You have lice."

I must let you know that bugs, parasites, and pretty much anything that crawls with little legs are my worst fears. To hear that I had lice—for the first time in my life at the age of twenty-one—was a hard blow. It was as if one more comfort had been stripped away from me as I served in this country alone. I didn't have fellowship, I didn't have English, and now I didn't even have physical comfort.

That morning, I sat at the breakfast table, crying and wanting with all my flesh to buy a ticket and go home. I couldn't do this on my own. I honestly did not want the girls to come to the home and be around me anymore; I didn't want to hug them, just in case I got lice again.

I turned on a worship song, and God did some serious talking to my soul. That song has a line that changed my entire mindset, as it says that there's nothing too dirty for the Lord that He cannot wash it clean. In that moment, God flooded my soul with empathy and conviction so hard I could barely hold my head up. In that moment, He gave me a look into how all those girls felt, physically, emotionally, and spiritually: dirty.

I immediately asked the Lord to forgive me for being so selfish and for even contemplating ending what He had started there. "Forgive me for thinking badly about those girls. Forgive me for even thinking about not extending love to them."

When they came to the house that day, I hugged every single one of them. I was not going to allow one attack hinder the impact of God's love. Yes, I battled lice the entire trip. Yes, I had to brush out lice eggs by myself every night before bed. Yes, I put every home remedy imaginable on my head to get rid of the lice (including hand sanitizer).

But God taught me what it means to be broken and simultaneously heal through my brokenness.

By being broken for a season, I was able to walk with girls who had been broken in much more severe ways. By allowing brokenness to touch my life, God was able to serve through me, touching the lives of girls who needed to feel His love. By allowing fear and anxiety to touch my life for a season, I was able to walk in empathy with the girls, almost all of whom struggled with fear, anxiety, and panic attacks in that home.

I'm not saying God gave me anxiety. I am saying that God uses the broken places in our lives for His purposes. When we hand them over to Him in surrender, we can trust that He will perfectly place the puzzle pieces back together again. I felt too broken for Him to use me, but now I understand that I couldn't have gone to Guatemala in any other way.

You may be feeling broken in this season of your life, as if there is no hope and that there is no way that God could use this season for any good. But I want to encourage you to surrender it to Him, and allow His perfect hand to paint a new portrait and make beauty from your brokenness.

Jesus came and was broken for us. He was perfect but came to earth and had to deal with the brokenness of humanity. Had He not done it for us, we would never know the salvation of God. Your brokenness may be the puzzle piece for someone who needs to know that God can redeem, restore, and heal. Allow what the enemy intends for evil to be turned around for the good by God. And remember that you are never too broken to shine the light and touch others' lives.

CHAPTER 4
Clearing the Cobwebs

Have you ever gone on a hike and been the first person in line? If so, then you will understand the term, "clearing the cobwebs." Often, when being the trailblazer of a hiking group, you are the one who clears the spiderwebs and cobwebs that had been placed for a season. You lead the group and continuously walk into webs, swatting their sticky lines away without success. While you are covered in the webs and feel the exhaustion of fighting their covering, those who follow behind you smoothly make their way along the path. It doesn't really seem fair, does it?

I went through some tough trials and felt like God would use every trial I had to help someone else. One time, I went through a strange and somewhat random season of doubt. It felt as though one day, I was on fire for God, and the next, I was fighting hard against doubt and unbelief. I lay on my dorm bed and cried in frustration because I felt like I could not break free of the questions. It was so stressful that I even spent a pretty penny on an Apologetics Bible, which helped to defend the faith, hoping it would give me any weapons to use against the doubts plaguing my mind.

In the midst of that fight, I went to the movies with my best friend and was excited to get a distraction from my mind. When we left the theater, we ran into an old high school friend we had not seen in quite some time. He went to another college, and when we last saw him, he was quite strong in the faith and on fire for the Lord. However, we knew that he had been struggling with his faith at school because many of his professors were not believers.

We caught up as we stood beside our cars, talking and laughing for some time about our college experiences. Then the conversation somehow turned to faith and God. Our friend mentioned the many doubts he was having and the struggles he was facing with his faith. It was as though he was reading every doubtful thought and struggle that I'd had for the past few weeks. Right then, I felt the Holy Spirit on me. Immediately, the doubt lifted from my mind, and I was able to see what was happening. God had prepared me with a season of doubt so that I could help my friend in his time of need.

We talked for a couple of hours, and every time he disclosed a doubt, the Holy Spirit gave me the revelation. Then God told me to give him the Bible I had bought that specialized in apologetics and defending the faith. That one hurt a little bit because it was brand new and still smelled so good, but I was obedient and trusted that God would use it to help our friend find his way back again.

As I lay in bed that night, with my mind free of doubt and unbelief, I smiled and thought, *Wow, God loved him so much that He prepared me to help him.* Then, my smile turned to a frown as I thought, *Oh, does this mean I will have to suffer a lot in order to help other people?* For a time, I feared that God would purposefully make me go through trials in order to use me to help others. I finally learned, however, that trials are promised in our lives, but God is good enough to not let the struggle be a waste. He takes those things meant for evil and turns them into good, not only for our own lives but in the lives of others.

Many struggles and trials later, my best friend and I were sitting on my couch in my first apartment. I had been married for a about seven months and had just had a miscarriage. That miscarriage was the hardest thing I had ever been through and still is, to this day. My faith was hit very hard. I struggled to feel the love of God in that season and attempted to understand His will and purpose. My friend and I talked about life, and I shared some of my frustrations and doubts. I said something like, "I'm tired of the battles. I am ready for some rest."

My best friend looked at me and said, "I'm always encouraged by your battles. It seems like you always go through things first so that I can have help when I go through them."

I frustratingly spat back, "I'm tired of having to go through things to help others. I need the help for once!"

She looked at me lovingly and said something that has changed my perspective on battles to this day: "Katie, you're just clearing the cobwebs."

Sometimes, we go through seasons of trial and storm, not because we are personally being tested but because God wants to use what we learn to help someone else. Doesn't sound very fair, does it? When I complained to God about this notion, the Holy Spirit sweetly answered me, "You are more like Christ in your storm than when the sea is smooth." I immediately repented and understood that, as a Christian, we are not called to a life of comfort but of Christlikeness. And sometimes, to be like Christ looks like suffering for someone else.

Christ came and was wounded and punished for our transgressions. He didn't deserve the judgment, but He took it anyway. He cleared our cobwebs and paved the way for our salvation because He loved us. Now, instead of the punishment we deserve, when we believe, we get to rejoice in salvation and eternal communion with the Father.

> He personally carried our sins in His body on the cross [willingly offering Himself on it, as on an altar of sacrifice], so that we might die to sin [becoming immune from the penalty and power of sin] and live for righteousness; for by His wounds you [who believe] have been healed. (1 Peter 2:24 AMP)

Through our wounds, we too can heal. Often, we think being wounded, struggling, or broken cancels out our ability to serve or help anyone else. But like Christ, we are called to be trailblazers—people who run the race, clear the cobwebs, and set the path of freedom for those who follow behind us. It's time we ran our race with endurance and long-suffering, realizing that our purposes are much more about the love of God and others than about ourselves.

If you feel as though you are often clearing the cobwebs for others, then it's time to embrace that call on your life as a trailblazer for the Lord and stop complaining about the storms. How amazing it is to understand that God sees you in such a mighty way that He would use you to help others. I think it is beautiful that we can enter into the suffering of Christ, in that we can learn to lay ourselves down for others as well.

The next time you are going through trials, whether of depression, fear, anxiety, or brokenness, just remember that someone following you will be helped if you allow God to use your story for His glory.

The fear and anxiety I battled is what gave me purpose to help others who walked through it to be set free. Where many may feel like fear is a permanent part of their lives, God has called me to remind them that He is bigger than any fear and is still the God on the throne. If God called us to "Fear not," then we can trust that a life free of fear is possible.

CHAPTER 5

Fight or Flight: Making Decisions Off Fear

Much of my anxiety dealt with the fear of making wrong decisions that were not in the will of God. It showed up, usually, when I attempted to date someone and had little or no attachment to that person. When anxiety appeared, all I had to do was flee the situation, and that would take care of the fear.

Often, when it comes to dealing with fear or anxiety, our bodies have a natural fight-or-flight reaction—we either run away from the threat, or we stay and fight. Every time I had anxiety, I found a way to escape whatever it was that was causing it.

Anxious after a first date? Find something wrong with the person and stop talking to him.

Anxious about an upcoming trip? Find any reason to cancel or postpone it.

Anxious about opportunities or open doors? Find any excuse to not take them.

Although I didn't realize it, every major decision I made in my life was made from a foundation of fear. I didn't make a decision based on faith in the Lord or by being led by the Spirit; if fear was present in my mind, that meant it wasn't of God. My thinking was,

Because God doesn't give us a spirit of fear, if I'm afraid, then it must mean God does not want me to do it.

Clearly logical, right? No. The enemy has always used fear and intimidation to hinder the call on the lives of God's people. If he wants to stop you from pursuing your God-given purpose, you better believe he will send fear and intimidation to keep you quiet and paralyzed into uselessness.

Up until that point in my life, I lived in flight mode; God had to step in. We cannot be purposeful in the kingdom of God if we run from every battle and live in fear. God wanted to use this battle in my life to teach me to stand and fight, rather than flee; to pursue the will of God, regardless if fear attempted to silence and paralyze me. One of the reasons I was paralyzed was out of fear of not pleasing the Lord, but I was living a life that, ironically, was not pleasing to the Lord. Funny how that works, isn't it?

> But without faith it is impossible to [walk with God and] please Him, for whoever comes [near] to God must [necessarily] believe that God exists and that He rewards those who [earnestly and diligently] seek Him. (Hebrews 11:6 AMP)

As a child of God who professed trust in the Lord's plans for my life and His sovereignty, I was living in such a way that professed the complete opposite. Fear and anxiety were the hands that guided me, not the Lord. God needs us in a place of surrender to His will; that regardless of our emotions, we will follow His plans and fight the good fight of faith (not fear).

Thankfully (yes, you read that correctly), the Lord allowed me to enter into a fight from which I couldn't flee. When anxiety now tried to make me flee a relationship that I knew was a gift from God, I finally had to realize that anxiety was not the Lord's guidance; that fear was not always something that told me which way to go but was a signal that I was most likely approaching the will of God.

Satan attempted to make me fear that God would take my best friend from me if I was disobedient. By the term *disobedient*, I don't mean outright sinning; I believed it was any kind of step in life that was not in the perfect will of God. I knew this was an irrational thought, but I felt all the fear and anxiety the enemy threw at me, so I had no choice but to stay and fight.

The Lord gave my best friend to me during a certain time in my life. Had she not been there, I'm not sure where I would be today. When the world tried to pull me away from the Lord's plans for my life, my best friend was there to help steer me back to Him. We were soul sisters, and to this day, I believe our friendship has been God-ordained since the beginning of time.

I believe the Lord allowed the enemy to tempt me to flee this relationship because He knew I would fight. He knew I would know this could not possibly be from the Him, thus breaking that first root of believing fear was from God. For almost two years, I fought against the irrational fear that if God was going to take my friend away because of disobedience, it would be easier to just leave the relationship myself first to stop the pain. Anxiety was rampant within me, and every time we made plans to hang out, I had to fight the urge to flee or make excuses. Eventually, the anxiety began to dissipate, and I continuously clung to the knowledge that this friendship was from God, and I had to fight for it. What I didn't know was that I wasn't only being trained for the biggest fight of my life, but I also would have to fight for the soul of my friend.

During college, she learned how to live independently from her family and enjoyed the taste of freedom that life had to offer. Some of that led to friendships formed in college that led to some questions and doubts about the Lord. One of those friendships included some differences in belief systems. One friend believed in universalism and that there were many paths to God and that God didn't send anyone to hell. Although I could see part of the struggle my friend was going through, I did not see the whole fight her soul was waging on the inside. After a couple of years, I finally talked with her about the details of that season.

She stared at me in awe as I finished telling her about my fight for our friendship. She said, "Katie, if you only knew what I was going through. I believe if you would have ended our friendship, I would have chosen to walk away from God."

Sometimes, the attack of the enemy isn't so much about you; sometimes it's about someone who is connected to you. Sometimes, the enemy wants you out of the picture so that he can work out his plan in someone else's life.

Had I given in to fear and anxiety—had I taken the easy way out and run from what I knew was from God—my best friend could have lost her way. If the enemy could have made Moses flee, then God's people would have stayed in bondage and slavery. If he could have made Elijah stay in that cave, then false prophets and Jezebel would not have been dealt with. If the enemy can make you stay hidden and running from fear, then he can stop the purpose and impact your life will have on many others.

But in the glorious ways of the Lord, He not only helped me fight for her sake, but He trained me in a way that would prepare me for the fight ahead.

A little bit of time passed, and I stayed single, unwilling to attempt dating due to exhaustion from the battles. It seemed hopeless that I would find my spouse, to the point that I almost wanted to give up on the idea entirely. Then, I got a friend request on social media from a guy who had some mutual friends with me. I accepted and did a little stalking (you've done it too). I thought he was cute and seemed very funny. We developed a healthy "liking" competition, liking each other's pictures and posts in somewhat of a social media tennis match. I waited and waited for him to reach out and make a move, yet nothing happened.

Feeling hopeless, I complained often to God about there not being any faithful men of God who wanted to pursue serious relationships anymore.

"God, I'm tired of being lonely. I want the man you have for me." After a couple of months, he finally sent me a message, which was simply an animation of a bear waving hi. I read the message and smiled to myself, thinking that he must be really shy and unsure how to start the conversation. I messaged back, and we began learning a little bit about each other. Any time the conversation would gear towards meeting in person however, anxiety started to rise. *Here we go again*, I thought.

Once again, I allowed myself to drift away and gradually pull myself away from him. I stopped talking to him and sank back into hopelessness, sure that I would never be married because of fear and anxiety.

One day, I was scrolling through my social media and came upon his Easter picture. My heart fluttered and then sank into disappointment. The Lord stopped me instantly: "That could be your husband, and you are going to allow fear to stop you." Had I not said I wouldn't make fear-based decisions any longer? Had I not just told my friends that the Lord was teaching me to step out in faith and follow Him, not fear? Was I going to go around the same mountain again?

I sent him a text and, thankfully, he responded. After that, we went on our first date and talked for hours. I hadn't enjoyed a date in so long. When I left, I was gleaming and excited and wanted to see him again as soon as possible. But the drive home alone left time for my mind to wander into old territories of fear. *What if I get hurt again? What if he isn't who God has for me? What if God gets mad at me for dating him? What if I mess up again?* Every question and fearful doubt crept in, and I found myself an anxious puddle once again.

I got home, and my brother asked me how things went.

"It was amazing but now I feel so anxious."

He simply looked at me, smiled, and said, "You are just experiencing a little PTSD. You have only ever experienced anxiety after dating, so because you were expecting it to show up, you thought yourself into it."

It made so much sense, but it didn't take the fear away. I took a shower and sat on the shower floor, letting the water hit me. "God," I said, "I will not let fear guide me in this. I will pursue him until you tell me otherwise. I want your will for my life, not my own. I trust you."

For the first time, I was going to let God lead me, not my emotions. I felt peace and took another step. We went out again a day later, and he met my all my friends at once (pretty brave on his part). Everything flowed so beautifully that it felt too good to be true. Every time fear would try to creep up, I went to the Lord and told Him to take the lead. Something was very different in this man. Many times, men would not take dating seriously or didn't have healthy sexual boundaries; they often were pushy with those. This man was the most respectful, trustworthy, honest man I had ever met. It sometimes even felt surreal to talk with him and realize that I didn't feel taken for granted or seen as an object.

I opened up to him about my battle with fear and anxiety, and he walked through it with me every step of the way. He prayed over me, led me, and spoke to broken areas of insecurities I didn't even know were still present from my past. We quickly knew that we had found the one our souls loved, and wedding plans began to emerge (even before an engagement; fun times, I know). I felt peace for quite some time—until my mother asked me one question: "Are you sure he's it?"

She didn't know that she was breaking open a dam of fear and anxiety; she didn't know that the enemy was using her to attempt to derail God's plans for my life. Because she had lived in caution and anxiety her entire life, being extra cautious was just a part of who she was. She only had asked a question, but that question was the first blow in the battle.

I went to bed that night and lay in the darkness, drowning in anxiety, fear, and questions. "Lord, I know he's from you, but I just

FROM CAPTIVE TO CAPTOR

- FROM CAPTIVE TO CAPTOR -

want to run. Please don't let me run." Tears fell down my face as I felt God's gift slipping from my grasp. I continuously fell back onto the Word of God, looking to Him for strength and endurance to continue forward.

During our six months of dating, I took each day as it came. Each day, I took a step of faith, staying in the fight instead of fleeing in fear. Each day, I held to the man God had given to me, knowing I would fight for him until the day I died. Although fear and anxiety attempted to silence and intimidate me, the Lord gave me enough strength and grace for each day to continue the battle. That was when I realized I couldn't let emotions be my compass. The Lord had spoken clearly on who this man was to me, and His Word was what I would stand on. It felt as though up until the day of our wedding, fear attempted to steal him away. But when we live in a life of surrender to the Lord, we can trust that His plans will prevail. When we continuously tell the Lord, "Have Your way," we can trust Him to do just that.

My wedding day was the most peaceful, wonderful, beautiful day of my life. The Lord had His hand so graciously on that day that I knew it was a gift specifically to me for staying in the fight.

I can say, without a doubt in my mind, that my husband has been the greatest gift to me from the Lord. Seeing the fruit of our marriage in such a short time has shown me why the enemy didn't want us to come together in the Lord. My husband has been the one to continuously push me in my calling, to push me past my fears, to call me out of weakness, and to lead me more into Christlikeness than anyone else ever has. Where others had left me broken and feeling worthless, the Lord used my husband's unconditional love and tenderness to help bring me back to wholeness.

Going through that battle of fear and anxiety led me to obtain the prize of my husband, and I would fight it over and over again. God has a plan for your life that is perfect, but that doesn't mean your life will always look perfect. It does mean, however, that His plan is worth fighting for. Fight past those fears and anxieties that try to paralyze you. Fight past those insecurities and doubts about being able to stand in the midst of battle. When you surrender to the Lord and His Spirit, then you can rest fully in the knowledge that He will fight for you. Everything I needed, He provided, and He will for you too.

Learning to fight rather than flee the battle is the greatest lesson I have learned thus far in my walk with the Lord. It gave me God-confidence; I know that whatever may come, He will embolden and strengthen me to fight through it. Does that mean I never feel fear anymore? Absolutely not. Fear will always attack the children of God, hoping to stop them from doing what He has called them to do. But it does mean that I no longer make fear-based decisions.

When I feel fear and anxiety raise their weapons at me, I no longer turn and flee. I stand my ground. I hold my shield of faith and my sword of the Word, and I fight. When fear tries to tell me which step to take next, I turn to the Spirit and ask Him where to go. My emotions are an addition to my life; they help me feel love, happiness, sadness, and excitement, whenever those are necessary. But my emotions do not have a say in which way I go in life because they are fickle and cannot always be trusted. No, my life is guided by the Spirit, who can be fully trusted.

I encourage you to ponder on your life. How many decisions do you make on a daily basis that are fear-based? How many times have you fled situations in fear when you should have stayed in the fight? Are you tired of letting fear have the final say? It's time to take steps of faith and follow the direction of the Spirit. I used to be confused by the scripture that says, "Seek peace and pursue it" (Psalm 34:14 NIV). I thought that meant if peace wasn't present, then I shouldn't continue forward. If that was true, then Christ would not have continued to the cross, and we all would be without salvation. In the garden, before the cross, Jesus did not have peace. He was so afraid that he sweated blood, but He prayed, "Not my will, Lord, but Yours."

Sometimes, we will not have peace, but that does not mean it isn't the Lord's will. What we pursue, then, is not outward, fleshly peace but peace in the Lord, and we know that if we follow His will, we will be OK. Jesus did not have peace in His flesh because He knew of the suffering that was to come, but He trusted and had peace in His Father. I did not have peace in pursuing my husband because the many fears of getting hurt and the unknown tried to derail the Father's plan. But I had peace in knowing that God's will would unfold in my life, as long as I trusted Him and continued forward.

> In all your ways know and acknowledge and recognize Him, and He will make your paths straight and smooth [removing obstacles that block your way]. (Proverbs 3:6 AMP)

I want you to truly be led by the Spirit in your life and not be led by fear. Continuously let your mind be filtered in the Word, and let your decisions be based on your faith and the truth in the Word, rather than on your own understanding or your emotions.

God is calling us to a place of faith-based living and calling us out of fear-based decision-making. Stop fleeing, and begin your fight today.

CHAPTER 6
To Fear Is to Believe a Lie

Fear will attack every person in some way throughout his or her lifetime, but I have learned that although fear is not rare it is a very specific attack. It is unique to every person and often individualized in such a way that whoever is battling the fear often believes he or she is the only person to ever experience it. My fear, which led to my fight with anxiety, was rooted in the fear of disappointing God or being punished by God. That root of fear branched out into a range of many unique fears—from missing a single church service, to going on a date, to seeing a movie at the movie theater. Every fear I had was somehow rooted in the fear that God was going to punish me if I wasn't perfect or if I failed Him—even if I failed Him accidently. This served to paralyze me and led me to live in a constant state of fear or to isolate myself completely so that I didn't have to face any triggers to my anxiety.

People fear many different things, such as dying, being alone, suffering, or sickness. Some fear losing people they love, never achieving their dreams, being stuck in life, or always being poor. I may have touched on some things you fear, but I also know that you may be dealing with fears that are very specific to you. I had specific fears that attacked me because they knew where I was vulnerable.

Once, I fasted because I wanted to get my flesh in submission to God, but when I broke the fast, I was attacked by the irrational fear that if I stopped fasting, God would punish me. Even though I knew God was saying it was OK, fear attacked that vulnerable spot of weakness in my life, so much so that I almost developed an eating disorder because I was afraid to eat again.

Luckily, I had my undergraduate and graduate degrees in psychology and counseling, so I knew what was happening in my mind. Although it didn't make the fight any less painful, I forced myself to eat out of fear of what might happen if I continued down that path. All this is to let you in on a very specific fear I had to battle.

You may be battling something that seems specifically against you, maybe even something you're afraid to tell another because it makes you feel too vulnerable or maybe even shameful. Even though the enemy's attack feels very specific to you and your vulnerabilities, there is a God who knows you more intimately than anyone or anything, and He promises to never forsake you or abandon you.

Sometimes, we are so afraid of the attack of the enemy that we forget the God that we serve. True, the enemy "prowls around *like* a roaring lion, seeking someone to devour" (1 Peter 5:8 AMP, italics added), but in the midst of the battle, we forget to remind ourselves that we serve the Lion of the tribe of Judah (Revelation 5:5 AMP). Where scripture says that the enemy is *like* a lion because he has to act intimidatingly, we serve a God who is *the* Lion, who will not leave us defenseless.

If God knows the number of hairs on your head (Luke 12:7 AMP), then you better believe He knows the specific fears you deal with, and He will not leave you alone in your battle. Finally, I stopped allowing myself to be attacked like a defenseless sheep and ran to my Shepherd, who was standing by my side. Sometimes, we listen so much to the attacks of the enemy that we forget to ask God what He has to say about it.

I was driving home from school one day, being bombarded in my mind by every fear imaginable. It was so bad that my head was hurting. Finally, I stopped listening to my thoughts, and I asked,

"God, what do you have to say?" Immediately, it was as though God said, "Finally!" He stilled my mind and spoke to me for the remainder of the drive home. He spoke His Word. He told me my identity in Him. He told me how much He loved me, and He spoke against every fear that attacked me with His promises and Word. It was as though, in one step of obedience, God was allowed to finally step in with His truth.

Sometimes, we get so caught up in the fight that we forget who is on our side. We are so busy complaining, murmuring, or even crying out to God that we never stop to listen to what He may have to say to us.

He is always speaking, and if you still your mind long enough to listen, you usually will find freedom waiting for you there. Did I still struggle with fear and anxiety after that experience? Of course. But I had found a tool for my arsenal in the fight against fear. From that day forward, when fear attacked my mind, I stilled it and listened to the Lord, and I let Him tell me the truth. Your feelings feel very real, but if they come against the Word of God, they are not true.

When Jesus was tempted in the desert, Satan attacked Him with scripture that had been twisted. Jesus used the truth of the Word to fight against Satan's attempts at deception. If you are battling doubt, fear, or unbelief—whatever the specifics of the fear may be—you need to run to the Word for complete truth. Had Jesus relied on what others had taught Him to help Him in His fight, He might have failed. We can't live off the faith of our parents, church, or friends in times of trial. Instead, we have everything we need in the Word. Go seek God and seek the truth, and when you find it, use it against the enemy when he attacks you. Fight like Jesus.

If you fear being loved by God, find every scripture you can on the love of the Father.

If you fear death, find the promises of God for you regarding death and everlasting life.

If you fear being sick, go to the Word and see how we are healed by His wounds.

If you fear being lonely, go to His promises that we are never alone and never forsaken and that He sets up relationships for us according to His will.

If you fear being punished by God, go to His Word and see how He took the punishment for our sins and justified us through His mercy and grace.

If you fear not being good enough, go to the Word and see that we are righteous in Christ and adopted into His family.

Stop being attacked by fears that try to hold you hostage, and instead, go to the truth and find your answers—and believe them. It takes as much energy to believe in the truth of the Word as it does to believe the lies that fear tries to make you believe. So then, choose to put your energy in believing and thinking on good things and the truth instead.

> Finally, believers, whatever is true, whatever is honorable and worthy of respect, whatever is right and confirmed by God's Word, whatever is pure and wholesome, whatever is lovely and brings peace, whatever is admirable and of good repute; if there is any excellence, if there is anything worthy of praise, think continually on these things [center your mind on them, and implant them in your heart]. (Philippians 4:8 AMP)

Fear is an attack to make you believe in something that is unseen, unexperienced, or unknown. It is a dread of something that is not yet here, an attack of a possibility and not a reality. When you can face the fear that is attacking you and acknowledge this truth, no matter how real the fear may feel, you are on the beginning steps of becoming free. Your mind is a tool that has to be reset. Reset it with the truth, acknowledge when an untruth attempts to come in, withstand it, and speak to it, and you will experience freedom.

So submit to [the authority of] God. Resist the devil
[stand firm against him] and he will flee from you.
(James 4:7 AMP)

When we submit our minds to God's truth and resist the
temptation to answer fear when it knocks on the door, the enemy
will flee from us. It's a promise of scripture. The fight against fear
and anxiety is not easy, but it isn't any harder than living in fear and
anxiety. Take up your sword (the Word), and stand firm against the
enemy's attacks. Freedom is available to you!

CHAPTER 7

Becoming a Prisoner of Hope

Hopelessness often accompanied my fight with anxiety and fear. It is so easy to be in the middle of a stormy season in life and believe that things never will change. It is easy to believe there will never be another light on the horizon or clearing in the clouds. Of course, this is not true, but it is a very convincing lie that is easy to accept when you are being bombarded from all sides.

After what felt like an eternity of fighting fear and anxiety, I sank into a place of numbness. Anxiety no longer directed my life and choices, but it kept me hidden in a cave for far too long.

In 1 Kings 18 and 19 we read a story about the prophet Elijah, who had just showed God's might in defeating the false prophets of Jezebel. When Jezebel claimed she would find him and kill him, however, he ran in fear and hid in the caves. He went from the heights of faith in his God to the depths of fear and hopelessness. When God asked Elijah why he was hiding, Elijah proclaimed that Israel had turned from God and that people were after his life. God told him to return because there were still seven thousand who had never bowed down to another god. He was not done yet.

Fear is an attack of the enemy on your life to keep you silent and hidden. If the enemy can shut your mouth and hinder your calling, then he has succeeded. I ran from anxiety and fear and into a cave, which I like to call *hiddenness*. I believed if I just didn't feel anything or chase after any calling and if I became complacent in my walk with God, then maybe I would be left alone long enough to "heal" from that long fight of anxiety and fear. What I thought was self-protection was really cowardice—hiding from the enemy in a state of hopelessness.

I went on this way for about a year, the first year of my marriage. I went to work, came home, made dinner, watched television, and did it all over again the next day. Every now and then, I would read the Word, but that often caused me to have anxiousness about what would happen if I got too close to God again. So I would run back to my cave and continue being numb, continue in hopelessness, and continue not living.

One day at the beginning of the next year, I lay in a bubble bath, immersed in water yet so thirsty for His drink. I closed my eyes, breathed in some courage, and spoke to God. "Lord, I need You. I need a change. I can't go on like this. I feel so dead inside. I want to feel again. What do I do?" I was desperate. Tears flowed down my face until they met the water as I waited for a reply from the One I needed most.

Finally, I heard the softly spoken words that changed my life in a mighty way: "Be a prisoner of hope."

Ah, there it was. That word—hope. I hated that word. Through my fight with anxiety and fear, the enemy had planted a seed of hopelessness and bitterness in my soul. Because I was not delivered in the way I had imagined, I had allowed a disappointment and anger toward the Lord to form in my soul. The only way to fight those feelings was to lose all hope. And that is what I had done up to that point. And here God was, asking me to hope again. It felt like a slap in the face.

I knew that I had read those words in scripture at some point, so, injured but desperate, I googled where it was.

Return to the stronghold [of security and prosperity],
O prisoners who have the hope; even today I am

declaring that I will restore double [your former prosperity] to you [as firstborn among nations]. (Zechariah 9:12 AMP)

As I read those words, a crack formed in the foundation of hopelessness in my soul. A gleam of light peeked through as my soul felt a drop of hope for the first time in a long time. *Restore double? Is it possible that God will restore everything the enemy has stolen in these last few years?* As soon as the thought crossed my mind, I threw it down. *No way, I don't want to be disappointed again. I would rather not hope for restoration than be disappointed.* I tucked that lesson away in my mind and went to bed again in my cave of hopelessness.

The Lord never leaves us alone, and I love that about Him. He doesn't leave us in the cave to die or in the miry clay to suffocate. Even though I was hiding, He still chased me. His love drew me out. Every day, He reached to me a little more, and that crack that formed that night began to grow. I decided it was time to retrain my mind—when hope tried to enter, I would let it stay. After all, it was just as easy to have hope in something good as to worry about something bad.

If fear has told you it is safer in your hiding place, it is time to come out. It is time to answer His call. Where you, like Elijah, see no hope in where you came from, God sees reality. Where Elijah thought all was lost in the Israelites, God still saw the faithful remnant. All is not lost in your life. What the enemy has stolen, God *will* restore. It's His promise, and He is faithful to keep His promises (Hebrews 10:23).

Just yesterday, my husband and I were walking the neighborhood, with our baby in the stroller. A month before we had our first son, we bought my childhood home as our first house. It was interesting to walk those same streets, making new memories where so many other memories had been made.

I thought of a time when I was fighting anxiety, fear, and hopelessness so bad that I had to get out of the house for some fresh air. So many bombarding thoughts and fears had plagued me that I had felt like I was smothering, and I had cried out to the Lord, "Please deliver me from this or take me. I can't live like this anymore."

I told my husband about that time as we walked, and he replied, "Thankfully, He didn't."

Hopelessness acts like fog on a mirror. It stops you from seeing things clearly and truthfully. I saw no hope for my future and no point to my life. Little did I know that months later, I would be walking victoriously, meet my husband, and, through that marriage, bear two sons. It was such a dreamlike moment—walking and reliving memories of what felt like someone else's life. I breathed in the goodness of God. Beside me walked a promise I never thought would come and a son I thought was impossible (and later, another son).

We cannot see what our future holds. Had my wishes for death come true, I would have missed everything that God had in store for me.

Hope. It's such a hard concept to grasp in the darkness. You may not remember how to hope, but I encourage you to try. When you plant a beautiful flower in your garden, you do so with the anticipation that it will take root and flourish in beauty and might. Hope is the same way. We do things, think things, pray things, and believe in things that we hope will be evident in our lives one day. But one thing we have that others may not is someone in whom to have hope. We can afford to make expensive hopes because we have a God who is known for doing things above and beyond all we could ask or pray or maybe hope for.

> Now to Him who is able to [carry out His purpose and] do superabundantly more than all that we dare ask or think [infinitely beyond our greatest prayers, hopes, or dreams]. According to His power that is at work within us, to Him be the glory in the church

and in Christ Jesus throughout generations forever and ever, Amen. (Ephesians 3:20 AMP)

It is possible to become a prisoner of hope. You have been hiding in a prison of fear, anxiety, depression, hopelessness, bitterness— you are used to being chained to something, whatever it may be. What a relief to know that God can take us from those chains of bondage and make us prisoners only of one thing: hope. Hope in His promises. Hope in His faithfulness. Hope in His ability to restore, redeem, and reroute our lives.

Although you may have gone into hiding, you are not hidden to Him who sees you. He sees, and He knows, and He loves, and He chases. I encourage you to stop running. Stop hiding. Stop stuffing your emotions and feelings, and feel again. Breathe again. Hope again.

For I know the plans and thoughts that I have for you' says the Lord, 'plans for peace and well-being and not for disaster, to give you a future and a hope. (Jeremiah 29:11 AMP)

PART 2

Battle Strategies

CHAPTER 8

Discerning Voices

When I was battling fear and anxiety, I craved hearing from anyone who had been through the same thing and come out on the other side. It was easy for others to simply give me advice; it wasn't necessarily wrong, but it just was not helpful. If you've battled fear or anxiety for any time and have been open with others about your struggle, you probably have heard the same phrases I heard, over and over:

"Just don't worry about it."

"Just don't think about it."

"You are so blessed. You should be thanking God and not thinking about your problems."

And the most popular, "Just trust God."

As I said earlier, none of that advice was wrong—each comment had inherent truth—but none was helpful. If you have been through a fight with anxiety and fear, you understand that sometimes it seems impossible to get out of the battle in your mind. No amount of trusting God or just being thankful takes away the feeling of dread and despair and constant fear.

I just wanted someone to tell me the key to fighting this battle. I needed help decluttering my mind from all the voices of fear, anxiousness, worry, and doubt so that I could find the voice of God and the truth of it all. That person never came along for me. It was a tough season of loneliness, weariness, and battling. But as I went through it, I told the Lord that if I ever had the chance to help others out of their pits, I would be there. I would be the person I wanted when I was fighting.

I have wanted to set the foundations for my story of fear and to show you the roots and foundations from which your fear might be growing. But I don't want to leave you with just the knowledge and understanding of what fear is and where it came from. I want to teach you the tools God gave me to get rid of fear, once and for all.

Let me be the one who tells you: I know what you're going through. I know how hard the fight has been for you. I know how tired you are. But let me give you hope. I've been there, and I have come out on the other side. This is how I did it.

When I first prayed to the Lord when I was fighting fear, my prayer was that the Lord would give me battle strategies against the enemy. I prayed that He would give me the discernment and wisdom to know who was placing thoughts in my head and what to do with them. According to the *Oxford Dictionary*, discernment is the ability to judge well. Precisely in biblical understanding, discernment is the ability to obtain spiritual guidance and understanding, often in the absence of judgment.

Discernment in people and situations often plays out as discerning realities that are not obvious to one's perception. An example for everyday life is when you meet a new person who seems really nice and put together, but you discern something underneath the façade. It is different from judgment of character because God often gives it to us so that we will have the knowledge that will help us make good relational and situational decisions. In dating, spiritual discernment is a wonderful tool the Lord can give us to sift through those who say the right things and have the right fruit.

In Philippians 1:9–10, Paul states,

> And this I pray, that your love may abound more
> and more, with knowledge and all discernment, so

that you may approve what is excellent, and so be pure and blameless for the day of Christ. (ESV)

But solid food is for the mature, for those who have their powers of discernment trained by constant practice to distinguish good from evil. (Hebrews 5:14 ESV)

For the Word of God is living and active, sharper than any two-edged sword, piercing to the division of soul and of spirit, of joints and of marrow, and discerning the thoughts and intentions of the heart. (Hebrews 4:12 ESV)

Do not be conformed to this world, but be transformed by the renewal of your mind, that by testing you may discern what is the will of God, what is good and acceptable and perfect. (Romans 12:2 ESV)

The natural person does not accept the things of the Spirit of God, for they are folly to him, and he is not able to understand them because they are spiritually discerned. (1 Corinthians 2:14 ESV)

But test everything; hold fast what is good. (1 Thessalonians 5:21 ESV)

As you can see, discernment is mentioned quite often in the Word of God. This is because it is a necessary gift that we Christians should seek so that we may not be defiled in our understanding of God, our relationships, and our thinking. If you are unfamiliar with discernment, I urge you to research scriptures to build a foundation of understanding. Even if you think you understand discernment, you may think of it as a need to discern teachings on God and outside voices of influence.

But what if I told you that the ability to spiritually discern your thoughts and emotions holds just as much a weight as discerning outside influences?

We spend the most time in our days with ourselves. Regardless of whether your day is packed full of busy schedules or is a day of rest, or whether you have many friend dates or have chosen a day on your couch watching television, there is one person you can never escape: *you.* Imagine having a friend who constantly was negative, constantly told you fearful things that made you anxious, and constantly brought up bad memories and often made you feel guilty or shameful. Would you keep that person around? Probably not.

However, we tend to be that person in our own lives, as we constantly think on negatives, relive the past, or succumb to emotions of fear, anxiety, anger, and depression. We tend to think that it's just the way we were made; our personalities tend to be pessimistic or realistic. But scripturally, we are given clear directions on what our emotions and thought lives should look like, so why do we fail so badly?

I have come to understand that our failure is in our inability to discern just *who* is doing the talking. Someone once told me something that made a huge impact on my life: not every thought you think is yours. Sometimes, the Lord will speak to you through your thought life, and sometimes the enemy will plant thoughts that tempt you to accept them and believe them.

We know that Christ had to deal with the same situation. In all the Gospels, we can find the story of Christ being tempted by Satan in the wilderness. After being baptized by the Spirit and anointed for His ministry, Jesus then went to the wilderness to fast and was tempted for forty days. It is very possible that Satan showed up in the flesh and tempted Christ, but it is also possible that the battle was in His mind. When you read of the temptations of Christ in the wilderness, you realize that Satan used twisted scripture to attack the vulnerable places of the flesh of Christ. We know that Christ did not sin, but temptation is not sin. Because Christ came in the flesh, He was tempted in every way that we are tempted so that we would have a high priest at the throne who knows what we battle against (Hebrews 4:15).

Look at what Christ was tempted with—fleshly things (food) because He was hungry; identity issues (*if you are who you say you are*); and spiritual issues (tempting Christ to shortcut His purpose for an easier route and bowing to another, rather than to the Father). It's ironic that in all the temptations of Christ, Satan used twisted scripture to argue his points. This is where discernment plays a part. Had Christ not discerned the truth of the thoughts Satan threw at Him, He might have fallen prey to temptation. Had He just believed the thoughts because there was scripture (no matter how misquoted or the context), He could have forfeited His future and the future of humankind.

If Satan attacked Christ with twisted scripture and lies in His vulnerable areas, how much more will he attempt to attack you in the same way? It is absolutely necessary that one of the first weapons in your arsenal against fear and anxiety is discerning who is talking to you.

One of the scriptures Satan twisted in my battle with fear was, "The Lord gives and the Lord takes away" (Job 1:21 AMP). I feared if I disobeyed God, even accidentally, and did not stay in His perfect will, then He would take people away from me. And whenever I tried to fight against this fear, Satan would throw that twisted scripture at my mind.

The first time the Lord told me to discern my own thoughts, this thought came to mind. I said, "Well, Lord, Your scripture does say this, so I don't know what is true concerning this fear."

The Lord spoke softly: "Seek my truth."

I went to scripture, where truth is found, and read the content of Job. I was still a little wary on what that scripture meant for me, so the Lord sent me to James 1:17:

Every good and perfect gift is from above; it comes down from the Father of lights [the Creator and Sustainer of the heavens], in whom there is no variation [no rising or setting] or shadow cast by His turning [for He is perfect and never changes. (AMP)

I then read 1 John 1:9:

If we [freely] admit that we have sinned and confess our sins, He is faithful and just [true to His own nature and promises], and will forgive us our sins and cleanse us continually from all unrighteousness. (AMP)

And last, I read Zephaniah 3:17:

The Lord your God is in your midst, a Warrior who saves. He will rejoice over you with joy; He will be quiet in His love [making no mention of your past sins]. (AMP)

All of these scriptures fully expressed the character of the Father for me. This was my first indication that the thought was not from God because it did not fully align with scripture. Although it was based on one tiny scripture, which was misquoted, no other scripture backed up Satan's accusations of God. The rest of scripture showed a fullness of the Father that quieted the lie.

The second way I knew this thought was not of the Lord was its fruit. The fruit of the lie brought fear, anxiety, and a wrong belief about God. Looking back, that should have been my first signal that the thought was a lie.

Discerning our thought lives is being aware of the many thoughts that come through our minds daily and the reactions we have to them. If the same thoughts continue in your mind and often produce ungodly fruit in your life, then it's entirely possible that the thought is not of God but is the enemy, attempting to infiltrate your mind. Again: the first weapon you need against fear and anxiety is discernment.

Pray that the Lord will give you wisdom and make you aware of your thought life. We easily may think all day long without giving attention to what we are allowing into our minds. We go about our days, letting whatever thoughts stay that come to mind and never pay attention to the fruit.

Have you ever scrolled through social media and realized, about five minutes into it, that you feel anxious or depressed? Often, we receive messages from all around us, and without realizing what we're doing, we accept them and then feel the result in our emotions. It's time for us to be intentional about our thought lives and let the Lord lead us into wisdom and discernment; then we will discern what is right, true, noble, and of good report, and that will give the Lord glory.

Pray today that the Lord will give you wisdom and discernment.

> If any of you lacks wisdom [to guide him through a decision or circumstance], he is to ask of [our benevolent] God, who gives to everyone generously and without rebuke or blame, and it will be given to him. (James 1:5 AMP).

Concerning the spiritual gifts of God:

> And to another the working of miracles, and to another prophecy [foretelling the future, speaking a new message from God to the people], and to another discernment of spirits [the ability to distinguish sound, godly doctrine from the deceptive doctrine

of manmade religions and cults]. (1 Corinthians 12:10 AMP).

We know that if we ask in Jesus's name, it will be given to us (John 14:14 AMP), so you can trust that if you ask the Lord to help you discern your thoughts that He will help you do it.

One step to your growth in discernment is to stay in your Word. Knowing the scriptures will help you to fight against the misquoting of the scriptures. When we know the truth, it is easy to discern a lie! Another way to grow in discernment is to surround yourself with a group of trustworthy, godly people. Have close friends from whom you can seek counsel and understanding, regarding things with which you are struggling.

Sometimes, we need to escape the clutter of our own thinking and let the voice of reason—through someone else—clarify our sight. Seeking godly counsel is a biblical principle, and God can use it to help you discern right and true thinking.

Once you are working on discerning your thoughts and whether they are from the enemy or the Lord, then what do you do? The next weapon in your battle strategy against fear and anxiety is taking your thoughts captive.

CHAPTER 9
From Captive to Captor

Imagine this: two mighty armies are on a battlefield, one in gold armor and the other in black. They are facing each other, waiting to begin the battle, but the battle cry has not yet been given. Looking on this scene from above, you see a soldier of the black army sneaking toward the line of the gold army. *What is he thinking? He's going to get caught!*

You watch as the soldier continues forward, breaking the line of the gold army. Confused, you see them stand by, allowing the enemy to break their strength and make his way farther into their territory. *Why don't they capture him?* you think in frustration. Some in the gold army are too busy to notice him. Some see him but don't feel like going after him because he's too fast, and they are too tired. Others simply aren't aware that he is an enemy.

The soldier in black makes his way behind the gold army and begins building a stronghold. One by one, other enemy soldiers make their way into the gold territory, strengthening the stronghold and building higher and higher. Eventually, the gold army turn around and realize they are surrounded on all sides. How did that happen? How did such a strong army become infiltrated and defeated? It was easy. They did not take the enemy captive, so he was able to set up in their territories.

This is the visual the Lord gave me when I asked about taking thoughts captive. I had heard it my entire life but never really understood the how-to behind it. When we allow thoughts to go unnoticed, or we simply are too tired or even too lazy to do the work of minding our minds, we often allow the enemy to take up territory in our minds and build strongholds.

A stronghold, in a literal sense, is a place that has been fortified so as to protect it against attack. Often, enemy strongholds in battle are built in such a way that tearing them down or overtaking them is almost impossible. We too can have strongholds in our minds— towers of lies we have believed about God, ourselves, or others that were built by the enemy and defended for many years. Enemy strongholds in our minds are often a result of untested, undiscerned thoughts that we allow to take hold in our minds, and we never deal with them.

In my case, I had strongholds built on these lies: that God didn't love me, that He wanted to punish me, and that He was the one who had given me fear and anxiety. Regardless of what truths I heard, until I dealt with these strongholds, my immediate reaction to situations and struggles was filtered through these towers of the enemy.

When I dealt with a question of God's love, I immediately retreated to the stronghold that said I wasn't worthy of His love. If I failed in any way, I immediately ran to the stronghold that said God would punish me for my failures. Sometimes, we have strongholds of which we are not aware. Had you asked me back then if God loved me, I would have said *of course* and then would have quoted all kinds of scripture that proved it. But I was functioning on a system of thinking built on the wrong strongholds. These are the roots of fear, and these are what we have to tear down.

I began to battle fear and anxiety during my senior year of college. I was studying psychology, and one of my classes was on abnormal psychology. That's a lot of fun—to study the mind when you feel like yours is falling apart. Sad to say, every time I went to that class, I ended up with some sort of anxiety attack because it increased my belief that something was wrong with me and that it was unfixable. During that time, I dived deep into the Word, searching for any kind of answer that would help me out of fear. I read "fear not" over and over but never truly found the *how*. Then I read 2 Corinthians 10:3–6, and something began to break:

> For though we walk in the flesh [as mortal men], we are not carrying on our [spiritual] warfare according to the flesh and using the weapons of man. The weapons of our warfare are not physical [weapons of flesh and blood]. Our weapons are divinely powerful for the destruction of fortresses. We are destroying sophisticated arguments and every exalted and proud thing that sets itself up against the [true] knowledge of God, and we are taking every thought and purpose captive to the obedience of Christ, being ready to punish every act of disobedience, when your own obedience is complete. (AMP)

As I read that scripture, I saw the same imagery that God had shown me of the two armies on the battlefield. I saw that the battlefield of our warfare is actually in our minds, since the weapon that is given in this scripture is the destruction of arguments and the taking captive of thoughts and purposes of the mind.

I realized that it was through this process that the fortresses (strongholds) in my mind, of fear and anxiety, would be defeated. I didn't know, however, just how much work was required to take captive every thought. But hard work does not mean impossible work. When God gives us direction, we can trust that the outcome is possible.

After reading this scripture, I asked the Lord to please show me how to take my thoughts captive. Up to this point, I believed that I was just a victim of the thoughts that went through my mind, and there wasn't much I could do about it—perhaps you feel this way too. After reading that scripture, however, I went to my abnormal psychology course and heard something that changed my life.

One of my favorite things about studying psychology, or any subject, is that when I study things of creation, I am always brought back to the Creator. I love studying the mind because it helps me see deeper into the mind of the one who created us. For me, psychology has always been another avenue of finding out about the Lord. In my classes I often studied concepts discovered through the study of psychology that lined up clearly with the Word of God. I could see the Master at work throughout the centuries of our human attempt at discovering His creation.

On this particular day, we were studying different treatment options for disorders of the mind that often had symptoms of maladaptive thinking. In short, this meant "stinking thinking"— thinking that is negative-centered and can cause self-hate, self-harm, and self-destruction. One of the treatments is called cognitive behavioral therapy, which quite clearly is the human application of taking every thought captive. As I studied this treatment for the first time, it was as though God was showing me the answer to my questions of *how*. Isn't it amazing that the Lord works through so many things to bring us freedom?

Simply put, cognitive behavioral therapy is the process of recognizing maladaptive thinking and then answering those thoughts with the truth. For example, if I have the thought, *What if no one likes me? What if I don't matter at all?*, the next step is to recognize the wrong thinking, seek the truth to that thought in myself or my close friends, and then answer that thought with the truth, such as, "No, I have many friends and family who love me and support me. I was created with purpose and people like me."

When maladaptive thinking is about the Lord, we can capture those thoughts and answer them with the truth in scripture.

I love how the Lord develops individual communication styles with His children. Some people hear Him in the still small voice, some in nature, and some in images and metaphors. I am one of those whom God always teaches through images (like the battlefield and the train station). When I asked the Lord how to take captive these thoughts, He showed me the image of a little mouse running around my mind (thoughts). And He showed me grabbing the mouse by the tail and tossing it out. It may sound silly, but as I walked through the process of taking captive every thought, this was the image I used. When I recognized a thought as wrong, I imagined myself hurrying to grab that mouse's tail and tossing him right out of my mind. Then I would ruminate on the truth to that thought, instead of the thought itself.

I have taught this principle to many people who battled fear and anxiety. At first, they laughed a little but then developed their own tools.

My best friend came over for dinner one night and told me how she shared this imagery with her small group, which was discussing the mind and taking thoughts captive. She then told me the different exercises and images that the girls had developed to deal with wrong thinking. One imagined herself tossing the thought off a cliff; another imagined slamming the thought with a bat or hammer; and another imagined catching it, putting it in a box, and then laying it at the cross.

"Do you still imagine catching the mouse?" my friend asked.

"I actually don't," I told her. "After having practiced this biblical skill for years now, I have learned to simply take the thought captive and think on truth. But the mouse tail image was definitely the doorway God used to help me learn how."

We all have to begin somewhere, so if using the image of you taking your thoughts captive will help you, I encourage you to begin that process right now!

You might ask, "How do I become aware of my thoughts? It seems they just automatically happen and go by."

The answer is quite simple: become aware of your thinking.

You may notice that the first few days or even weeks of this process are emotionally exhausting, but eventually, you will become aware of how many thoughts, good and bad, run through your mind on a daily basis. When I began this process, my brain physically hurt from taking captive so many thoughts all day long. But if you stick to it, you will see freedom in your mind. You will notice that those thoughts don't have the same hold on you as they used to do. You will see the promises of peace unfold in your life.

Learning to take thoughts captive is exactly as hard as you might imagine taking captive those enemy soldiers would be. There is a fight to be had and a part to play. But God would not tell us to do something if He did not give us the strength to do so through *His* might. Ask the Lord to give you the ability and strength to recognize your thoughts and take them captive. He will help you, and you will understand that you don't have to live in bondage to your thinking any longer.

When we battle our minds, whether through fear, anxiety, depression, suicidality, self-hate, low self-esteem, or whatever it may be, we feel like we are quite captive ourselves. The freedoms of light-heartedness, joy, laughter, optimism, and love all seem so far away and impossible to reach. I've been in that hopeless place of feeling like there was never going to be normal again and that my entire life would be held captive and plagued by the darkness of anxiety and fear. Even if I did get married and have a family, I felt that anxiety would lurk behind every corner and steal whatever joy I did feel. These were lies—lies I had to take captive so that I no longer stayed in captivity myself.

God wants to take you from being held captive to being the captor. Where you have felt like you were in prison, God will show you that you are free indeed, and He will show you the power you have to shut down the enemy. Where you have felt like you have to remain in hiding in order to feel safe from the attack, God will show you that He will be your weapon, and He will destroy your enemy. All you have to do is be still.

Sometimes, we over complicate the Word of God. We mystify it and make it into a spiritual puzzle, and we hope that we can understand enough of it to get us through this life. We have the one who wrote the Word actively present in our lives, if we are saved and justified through Christ, so when we approach the Word and simply ask for revelation, He will give it to us.

You may think that the fears and thoughts you deal with aren't necessarily in the Word or that they can't easily be fought by the Word, so how do you know to take them captive? How do you know how to answer them?

The answer is quite simple. Scripture gives us a thought-filter system.

In Philippians 4:6–7, we are given a formula of action for when we feel anxious:

> Do not be anxious or worried about anything, but in everything [every circumstance and situation], by prayer and petition with thanksgiving, continue to make your [specific] requests known to God. And the peace of God [that peace which reassures the heart, that peace] which transcends all understanding, [that peace which] stands guard over your hearts and minds in Christ Jesus [is yours]. (AMP)

How beautiful. When you feel anxious or worried, pray to the Lord with specific requests; give thanks to the Lord for your blessings and His goodness, and then the peace of God will stand guard over your heart and mind. Try it! Remember: the next time you feel worried or anxious about something, pray to the Lord, give thanks, and you will find comfort and peace.

But it our directions for dealing with anxiety and fear don't stop there. In Philippians 4:8–9, we are given the thought-filtering system for every single thought that goes through our minds:

Finally, believers, whatever is true, whatever is honorable and worthy of respect, whatever is right and confirmed by God's Word, whatever is pure and wholesome, whatever is lovely and brings peace, whatever is admirable and of good repute; if there is any excellence, if there is anything worthy of praise, think *continually* on these things [center your mind on them, and implant them in your heart]. The things which you have learned and received and heard and seen in me, practice these things [in daily life], and the God [who is the source] of peace and well-being will be with you. (AMP)

If you have thoughts that don't fit the above description, it's time to take them captive. I will reiterate that the lie you believe—that you have to stay imprisoned to fear and anxiety—is simply that: a lie. God would not give us clear directive on not living fearfully or worried and then leave us that way.

When you look ahead at your journey as you walk through the decluttering process of your mind, don't feel that the giant is too big for you to face. Instead, feel hope and excitement as you realize you are beginning a journey that will lead to freedom and hope. You do not have to live in fear and anxiety. Mind your thoughts, take thoughts captive that raise themselves against the knowledge of Christ and what Christ says about you, and still your mind on His truth and Word. Peace will come.

You will keep in perfect and constant peace the one whose mind is steadfast [that is, committed and focused on You- in both inclination and character], because he trusts and takes refuge in You [with hope and confident expectation]. (Isaiah 26:3 AMP)

At the beginning of this chapter, I discussed how the enemy can have strongholds in our minds. As you work with the Lord to tear these strongholds down, I want to encourage you that you are not left alone in the battle. Psalm 18:2 says, "The Lord is my rock, my fortress, and the One who rescues me; My God, my rock and strength in whom I trust and take refuge; my shield, and the horn of my salvation, my high tower- my stronghold" (AMP).

You have a God who can defeat any enemy in your life and to whom you can run for cover. Where the enemy has placed strongholds in your mind, you have *the* stronghold as your Father. You can trust in Him as you walk. Trust His goodness, His plans, and even His processes.

It isn't easy, I have walked the path before, but trust me when I tell you that the fruits you will see from allowing the Lord to uproot wrong thinking and lies from your soul will be beautiful. It is worth the pain of pruning.

CHAPTER 10
The Sword of God

I have found that in my walk with the Lord, the strongest weapon I have against all attacks of the enemy is *not* in being a "good" Christian, *not* in doing enough spiritual things and checking off a to-do list, but in one simple thing: coming to know the character of God through His Word.

As I look back on all my fears, worries, unknown questions, doubts, and battles, the one thing that brought me victory was not anything I did but in everything that God *is*.

I truly believe that when we fully understand the character of God, all fears dissipate. When we truly know who God is and who He says He is, we can rest in that knowledge, and whatever may come our way, we will be just fine. Much of my battle would have been over if I had known the character of God. My knowing that He is a good Father who can be trusted completely dispels every lie that says otherwise. My knowing that He has a plan and purpose for my life and that I don't have to figure out every detail but simply trust in His timing would have completely abolished every fear that said it was up to me.

My knowing how much I am loved by the Father tells me that no matter what, I can do anything *through* Him. I don't have to have everything figured out. I don't have to know everything that is to come. I don't even have to know the whats, hows, and wheres; I simply need to know the who.

That's much easier said than done, especially since I believe we never fully know everything about God; that journey will continue into eternity. But that is why our first weapon is in what we were given to know God—His Word. His Word is where we meet Him and come to know who He is. His Word gives us direction for our lives and the guidelines to live by. His Word gives us the revelations we need for the battle we may be in. But it is not just full of all kinds of truth; it *is* the weapon of our warfare.

> For the Word of God is living and active and full of power [making it operative, energizing, and effective]. It is sharper than any two-edged sword, penetrating as far as the division of the soul and spirit [the completeness of a person], and of both joints and marrow [the deepest parts of our nature], exposing and judging the very thoughts and intentions of the heart. (Hebrews 4:12 AMP)

We don't serve a dead God who gave us a bunch of philosophies to live by. No, we serve a God who is very much alive and who has given us the weapon to defeat the enemy in our lives. Your main weapon against fear and anxiety and every other temptation the enemy may throw your way is the Word of God.

Imagine this: You are in the middle of a dry desert, with mountains surrounding you and dark clouds hanging above you. In front of you is the enemy, spewing lies about you, casting fear on you, and trying to intimidate you into surrender. You see you are wearing armor that covers your head, shoulders, torso, and legs. You also have a shield that can protect you from whatever comes your way. You feel good for a second, thinking you have everything you need for the battle—until the enemy pulls out a sword and approaches you for hand-to-hand combat.

You look down and see your hand is empty. You can defend yourself all day long but never serve any offensive moves. Eventually, you will tire out, and the enemy will conquer you. Many Christians today live this way. They carry the armor and even a shield of faith, but they lack the most important thing in battle: a weapon.

As Christians, we never must get so comfortable and content that we forget to sharpen our swords and be prepared for battle. I lived as a non-victorious Christian for too long. I took the punches of the enemy but never had the strength to strike back. I often felt pounded to the ground, holding my arms in front of my face, merely trying to survive the fight instead of fighting back. It wasn't until the Lord showed me the might He has waiting in His Word, which would prepare me for battle and lead me to victory.

You can try to fight off the enemy all day long, but until you take up your sword and live by it, you will feel defeated and exhausted from battle. The key to defeating the enemy of fear and anxiety lies in the Word of God. Pick up your sword, soldier, and yield it. You will no longer feel like the ant being stepped on; you will be the mighty warrior who yells victory.

We were promised battle. We were never promised a comfortable life of always fitting in, always feeling warm and comfy in our souls. It's time we lay down our fleshly wants and understand that we are in a battle, and it's time to fight back. God is taking us into a time of victory.

If you have felt defeated far too long, He will breathe new life into you, full of fire and strength. It's time to understand who the God you serve is and who He has made you to be.

You may feel too exhausted to fight back. You may say that you've been fighting way too long, and you would rather have a rest. But God wants to teach you how to fight from *His* strength, not yours. When we rest in the Lord, we can fight and still be at peace. Many times in scripture, the Lord tells us to be still.

Be still and know (recognize, understand) that I am God. I will be exalted among the nations! I will be exalted in the earth. (Psalm 46:10 AMP)

The Lord will fight for you while you [only need to] keep silent and remain calm. (Exodus 14:14 AMP)

My favorite one has to be the story of Jesus and the disciples in the midst of the storm. In Mark 4:35–41, the disciples and Jesus are crossing the Sea of Galilee and come upon a storm. During this storm, the disciples run about the boat, scurrying in fear, proclaiming that they are going to die. At the same time, our Lord Jesus is taking a nap below deck. The disciples wake Him from His sleep. He walks up on the deck and tells the storm, "Peace; be still!" Then Jesus asks why the disciples are so afraid and have such little faith.

This story is such a beautiful and even funny image to me. From the outside it appears as though the disciples had every reason to be afraid of the storm. But when we acknowledge who was with them, we can giggle a little at the thought of them waking Jesus and telling Him they were all going to die.

Hadn't Jesus told them they would cross over to the other side? Hadn't He said they had a purpose to fulfill? Yet at the first sign of turbulence, they ran in fear and forgot everything He told them.

God wants us to live in a place of complete rest so that when the storms of this life come, we can be still and trust in Him. We have to know who is on board with us. We are not sailing this life alone. When the storms and trials come, no matter how hard the wind is blowing or how painful the stinging rain may feel, we can run to God and trust that He still speaks to storms and commands them to cease.

You don't have to fear the storms and trials of this life. There is a place of rest in the Lord where you can find complete peace, no matter what may come your way. This was why all the disciples were able to be at peace, even when they were put to death. This was how Stephen was able to pray for those who stoned him and remain completely calm as death approached. This was how Paul was able to write half of the New Testament from the confines of a prison cell.

Come to know the God you serve and the God who is on board your ship; that is the answer to this peace and rest. Get in your Word, let it soak your soul, and bear your sword.

CHAPTER 11

The Lord Is Your Shepherd

> The thief comes only in order to steal and kill and
> destroy. I came that they may have life, and have it
> in abundance [to the full, till it overflows].
>
> —John 10:10 (AMP)

We often hear this scripture as a promise of a good life in Christ, that Christ came to give us everything we ever wanted, and we can live, prosperous and happy, forever.

While there are many times in this life when you will experience prosperity and joy, that is not the abundance of life that I believe Christ offers. The enemy comes to steal, kill, and destroy your life. He wants to steal your joy, kill your promise, and destroy the plans of God for you.

But Jesus came so that we can have abundance *in* Him— abundance of peace, joy, and purpose, as we need it. We have the abundance of love from the Father from whom we can never be separated. We have the abundance of peace that surpasses all understanding. And we have the abundance of joy when we acknowledge that the joy of the Lord is our strength.

You were not created to live a life of darkness, sin, and hopelessness. You were created for perfect communion with God, purpose, and light. When the enemy yells loudly—intimidating you, telling you that he will overtake you—that still small voice of the Lord proclaims that His plans for you are good.

We must come to a place of surrender in the Lord, and this place often brings about the fruit of peace in our lives. When we surrender our plans, expectations, and dreams and fall into the plan of God for our lives, we will find fulfillment and abundance that we never could have imagined.

> Now to Him Who is able to [carry out His purpose and] do superabundantly more than all that we dare ask or think [infinitely beyond our greatest prayers, hopes or dreams], according to His power that is at work within us, to Him be the glory in the church and in Christ Jesus throughout all generations forever and ever. Amen. (Ephesians 3:20–21 AMP)

When God asks for surrender, we can trust His character and know that what He has planned is infinitely better for us, no matter what it might look like. Whatever He might ask us to give up for His purposes, we can trust that it is for our good.

The image in the Word that has brought the most peace in my life is that of the Shepherd. I am going to share Psalm 23 in its entirety because we need to see it in its fullness.

Psalm 23 (AMP)

> The Lord is my Shepherd [to feed, to guide
> and to shield me], I shall not want.
> He lets me lie down in green pastures; He leads
> me beside the still and quiet waters.
> He refreshes and restores my soul (life); He leads me
> in the paths of righteousness for His name's sake.

Even though I walk through the [sunless] valley of the shadow of
death, I fear no evil, for You are with me; Your rod [to protect]
and Your staff [to guide], they comfort and console me.
You prepare a table before me in the presence of my enemies. You
have anointed and refreshed my head with oil; my cup overflows.
Surely goodness and mercy and unfailing love shall follow me
all the days of my life, and I shall dwell forever [throughout
all my days] in the house and in the presence of the Lord.

What an absolutely peace-giving scripture and image for us. We
have a good Shepherd who knows how to take care of us. We can
trust Him.

I am the Good Shepherd. The Good Shepherd lays
down His [own] life for the sheep … The sheep
that are My own hear My voice and listen to ME;
I know them, and they follow Me. And I will give
them eternal life, and they will never, ever, [by any
means] perish; and no one will ever snatch them out
of My hand. (John 10:11, 27–28 AMP)

How wonderful to know that our Shepherd loves us so that He
laid down His life for us. He holds us in His hand, and no one can
snatch us out. He is the one who guides and protects us. I wouldn't
want to be in any other place but the guidance of the Shepherd.

When you feel shaky, worried, or fearful and don't quite know
which way you are going, you can trust the Shepherd. Even if you
feel like you have messed up so greatly that there is no going back,
He still will come after you.

What do you think? If a man has a hundred sheep,
and one of them gets lost, will he not leave the
ninety-nine on the mountain and go in search of
the one that is lost? And if it turns out that he finds

it, I assure you and most solemnly say to you, he rejoices over it more than over the ninety-nine that did not get lost. So it is not the will of your Father who is in heaven that one of these little ones be lost. (Matthew 18:12–14 AMP)

I constantly lived with the fear that I would mess up my life so grandly that God would not be able to use me. Somehow, I thought, I would make a wrong decision that would hurt me or hurt God. But when I understood the Lord as my Shepherd, all those fears went away. As long as I continued to look forward to the Shepherd, He would guide me. As long as I surrendered my relationships and choices to the Lord, He would protect me. As long as I went to Him for my rest and consolation, He would lead me to still waters and peaceful pastures. As long as I remained in Him, none could snatch me away. And even if I did gravely mess up, He would leave the ninety-nine for me.

There is no fear in love. When we come to know that love is not an emotion but a person, we will realize that fear has no hold on us any longer. To be so fully, perfectly, and wonderfully loved by the Shepherd means there is no longer any cause to fear. His perfect love will cast it out.

Come to know Him as your Shepherd. Come and let Him reign in your life. It is possible to be saved yet not fully know the God who saved you. It is possible to be His yet still live in bondage to mindsets He wants to prune away. He wants to set you free today from everything that attempts to take your eyes away from Him. He wants to remove everything that bears weight on your shoulders. Now is the time to surrender everything, be still, and rest in the Lord.

Come to Me, all who are weary and heavily burdened [by religious rituals that provide no peace], and I will give you rest [refreshing your souls with salvation]. Take My yoke upon you and learn from Me [following Me as My disciple], for I am gentle and humble in heart, and you will find rest (renewal, blessed quiet) for your souls. For My yoke is easy [to bear] and My burden is light. (Matthew 11:28–30 AMP)

Isn't that what you crave—blessed quiet? Peace? Real love? Lay down the yokes you have been carrying and pick up His.

After you've read this book, I encourage you to first go to your secret place in the Lord and receive His yoke and burden. I want you to go to Him and be still. And then I want you to pray for His revelation on how to begin the journey of sifting through your roots and finding the whys behind your struggles. Then, start the process of discerning the enemy, taking captive every thought, picking up your sword, and trusting in the Lord.

I cannot promise you that your fear immediately will cease. It took me awhile and a time of self-discipline and steadfastness to finally see the fruit of the job. But please, hear my heart when I tell you it is worth it.

It is worth the hard work for your future. It is worth the hard work for those who come behind you, needing what you have to offer them from the Lord. It is worth it for your family and friends who want to see you live again. It is worth it for all those who watch you, hopeless, seeing what the Lord can do for them as well.

Take a deep breath. Steady your heart and mind. And fight like you know He is fighting with you.

Psalm 91 (AMP)

He who dwells in the shelter of the Most High will
remain secure and rest in the shadow of the Almighty
[whose power no enemy can withstand].
I will say of the Lord, "He is my refuge and my fortress, My God,
in whom I trust [with great confidence, and on whom I rely]!"
For He will save you from the trap of the
fowler, and from the deadly pestilence.
He will cover you and completely protect you with
His pinions, and under His wings you will find
refuge; His faithfulness is a shield and a wall.
You will not be afraid of the terror of night,
nor of the arrow that flies by day,
Nor of the pestilence that stalks in darkness, nor of the
destruction (sudden death) that lays waste at noon.
A thousand may fall at your side, and ten thousand at
your right hand, but danger will not come near you.
You will only [be a spectator as you] look on with your
eyes and witness the [divine] repayment of the wicked [as
you watch safely from the shelter of the Most High].
Because you have made the Lord, [who is] my refuge,
even the Most High, your dwelling place,
No evil will befall you, nor will any plague come near your tent.
For He will command His angels in regard to you, to protect and
defend and guard you in all your ways [of obedience and service].
They will lift you up in their hands, so that you
do not [even] strike your foot against stone.
You will tread upon the lion and the cobra; the young
lion and the serpent you will trample underfoot.
"Because he set his love on Me, therefore I will save
him; I will set him [securely] on high, because he knows
My name [he confidently trusts and relies on Me,
knowing I will never abandon him, no, never].

He will call upon Me, and I will answer him; I will be
with him in trouble; I will rescue him and honor him.
With a long life I will satisfy him and I
will let him see My salvation."

Printed in the United States
by Baker & Taylor Publisher Services